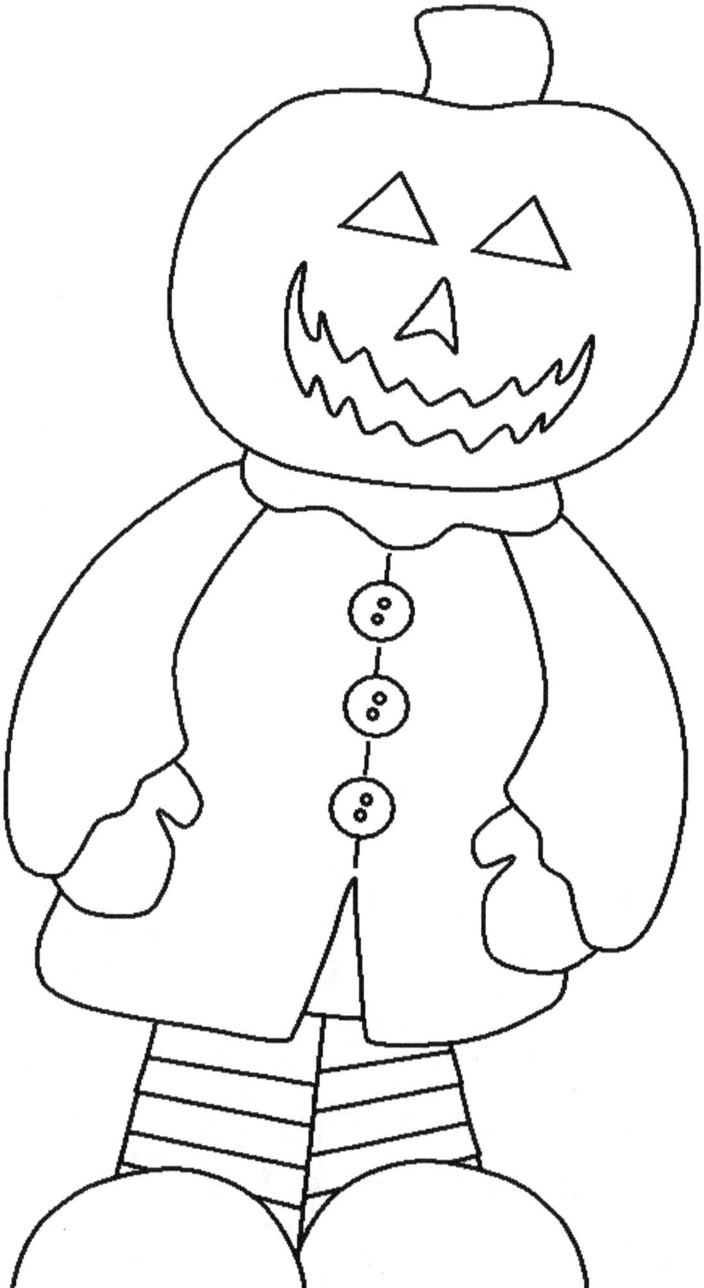

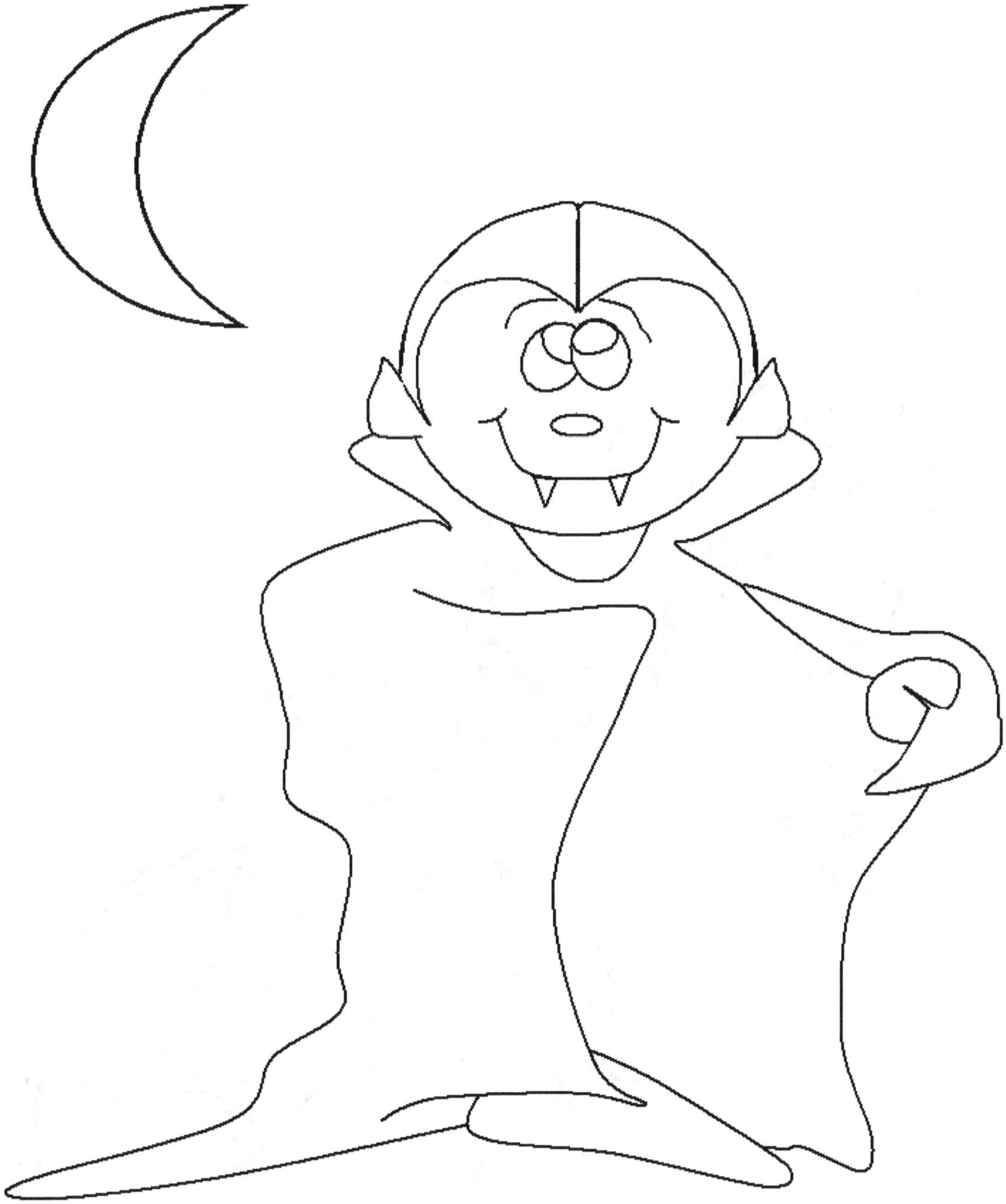

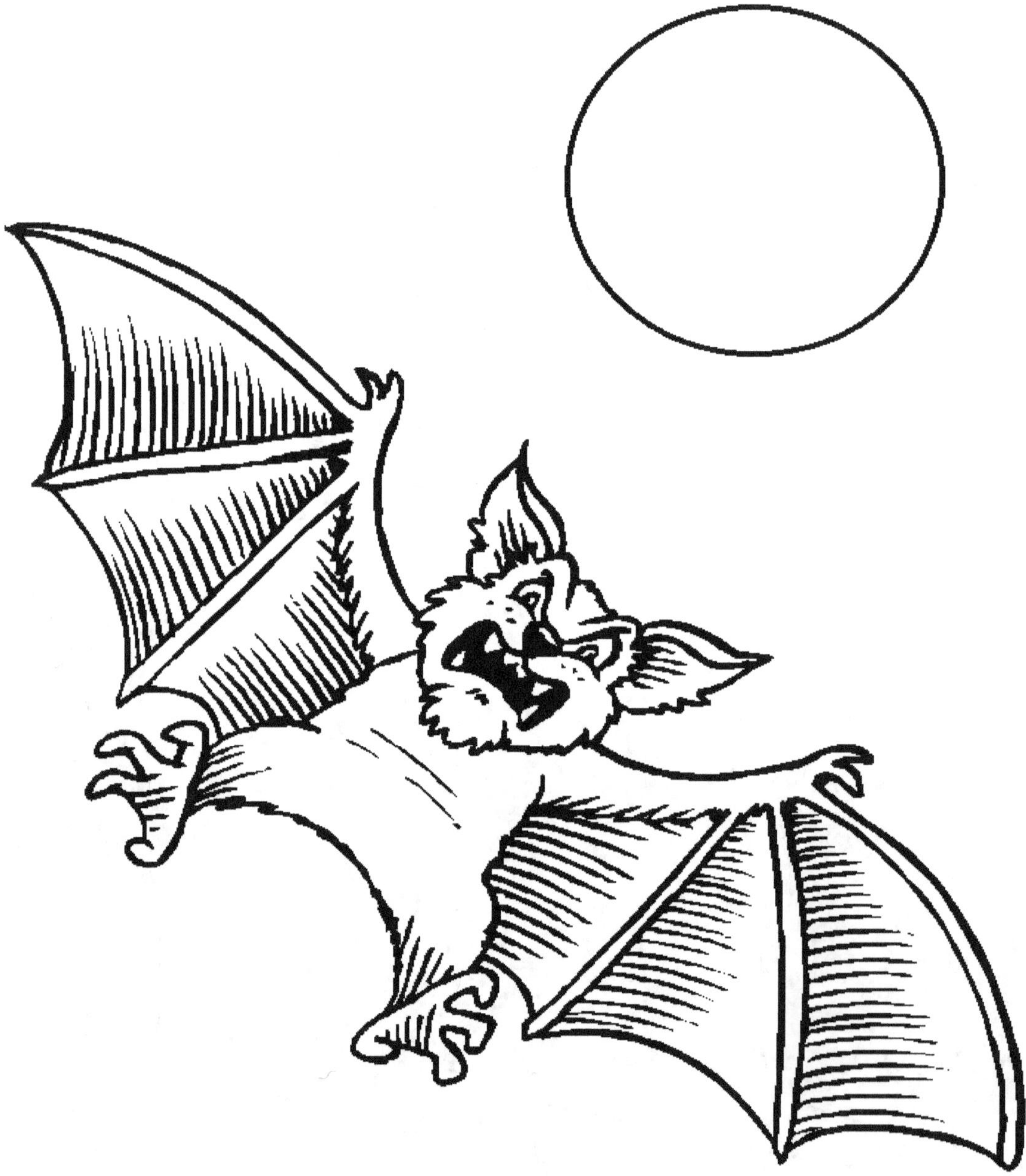

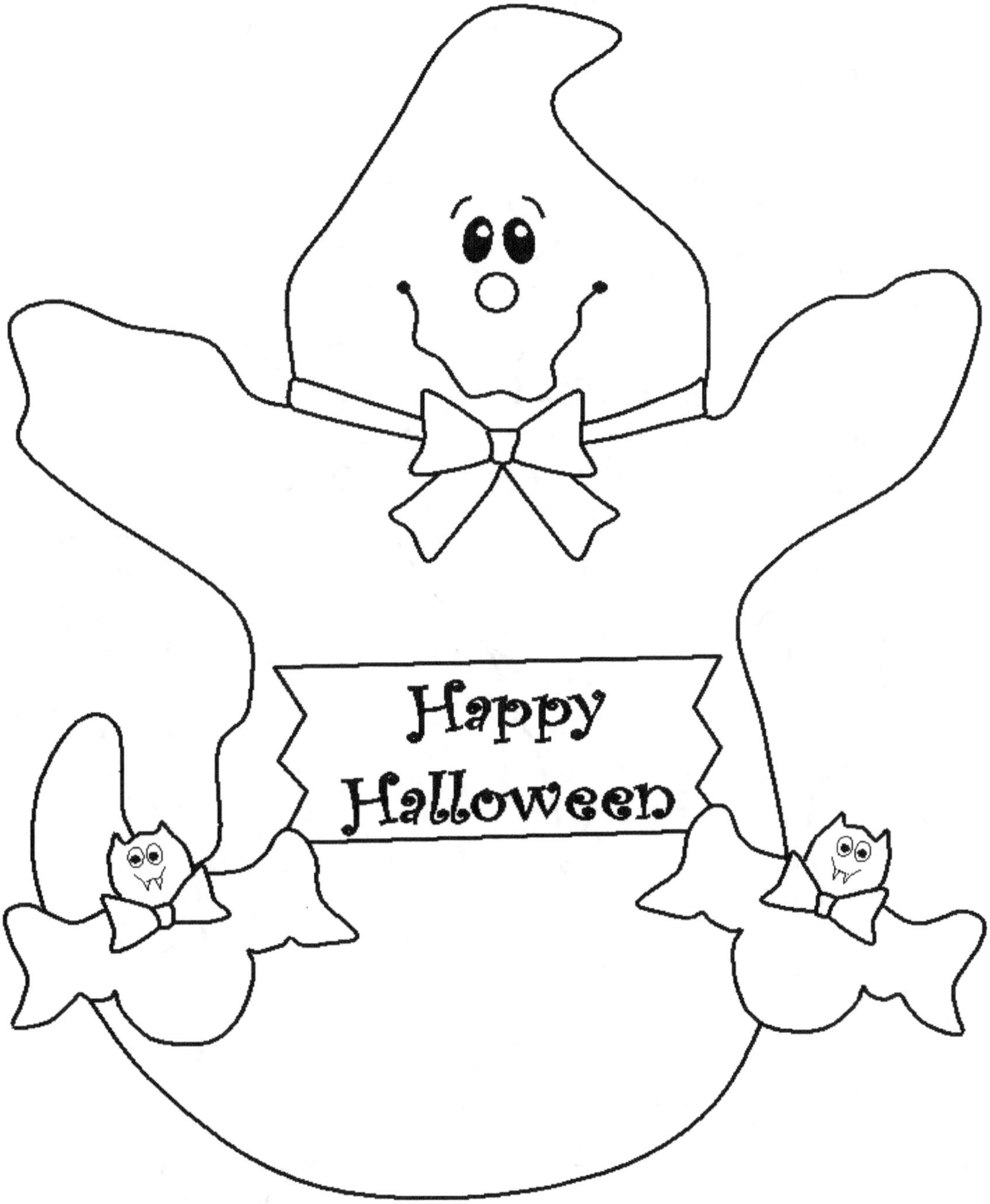
Happy
Halloween

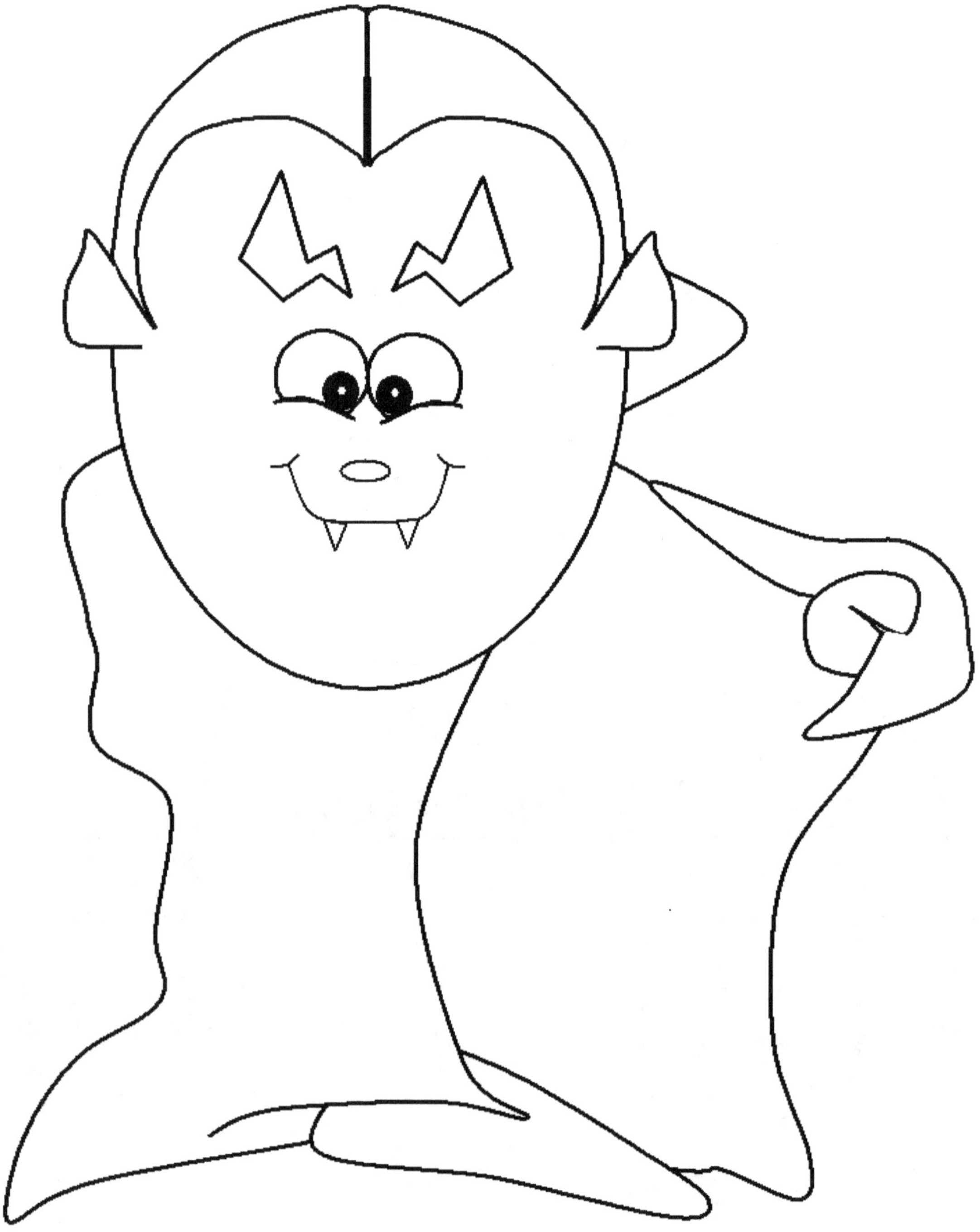

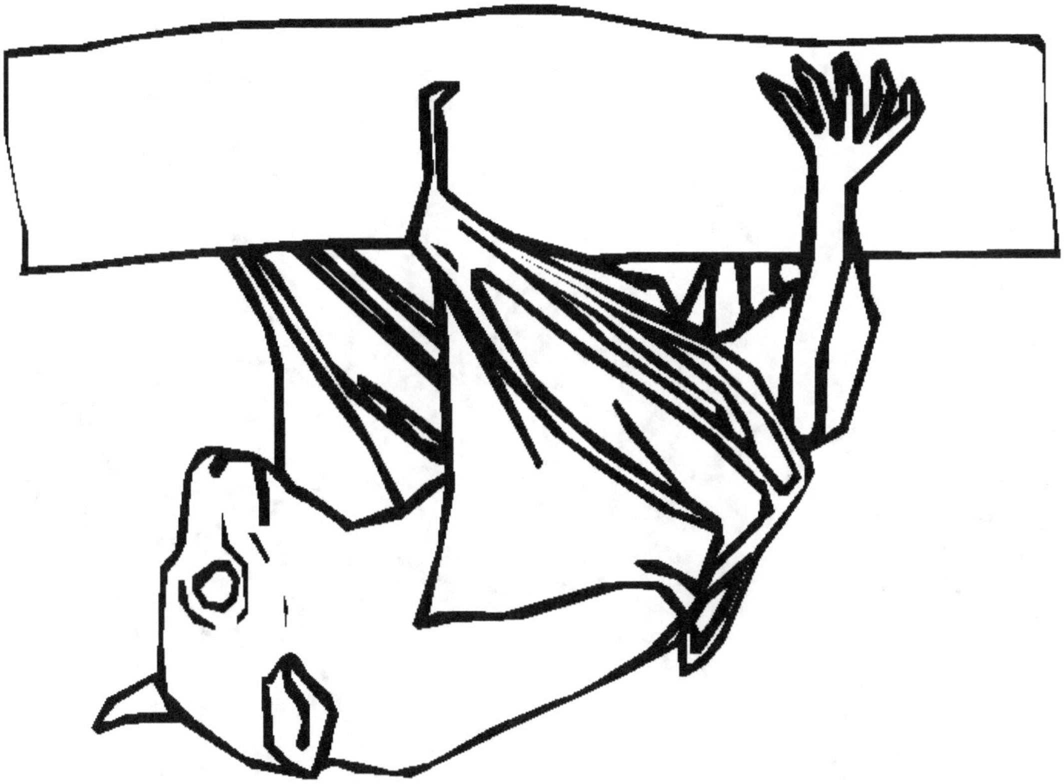

Just Hangin' Around!

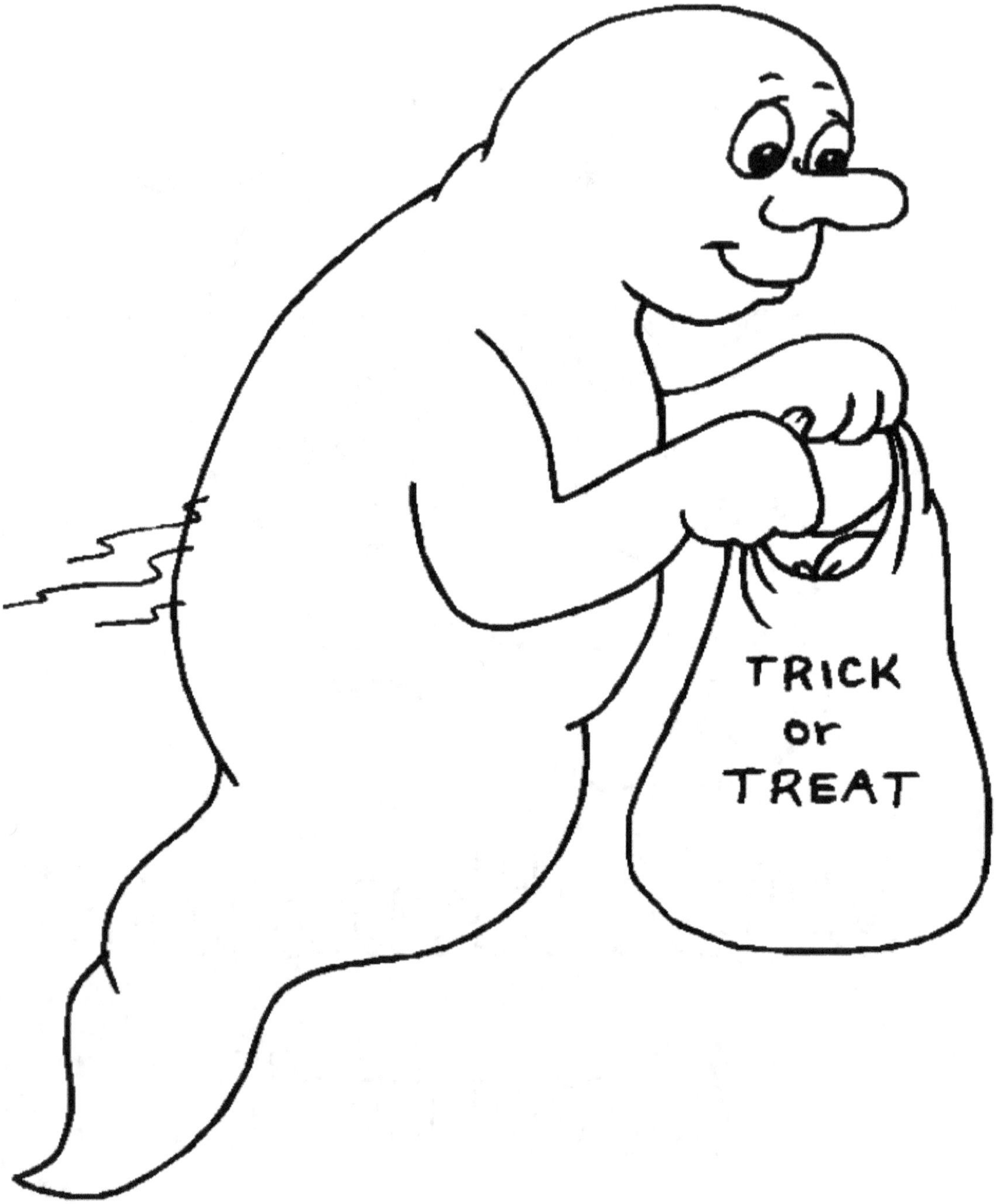
TRICK
or
TREAT

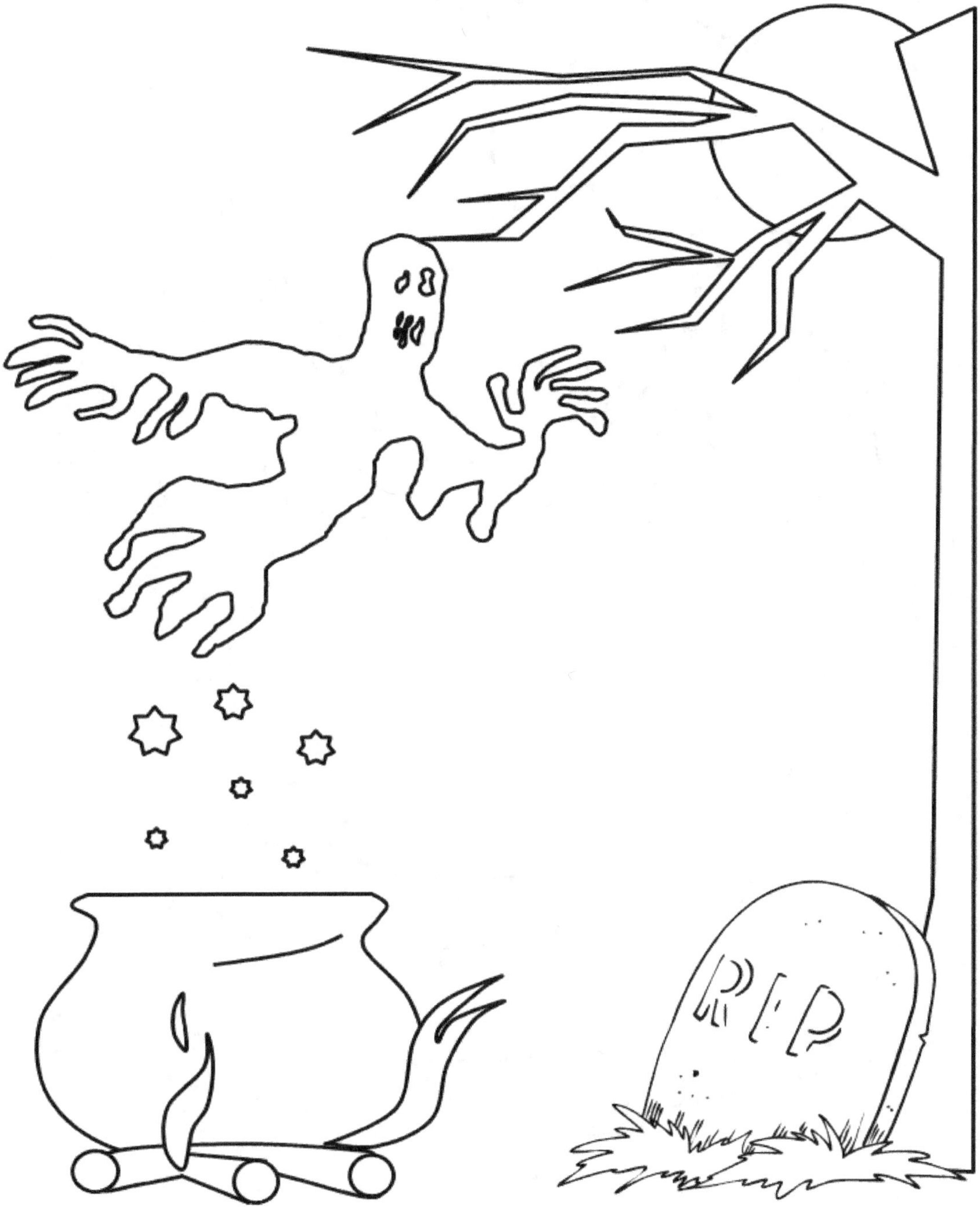
RIP

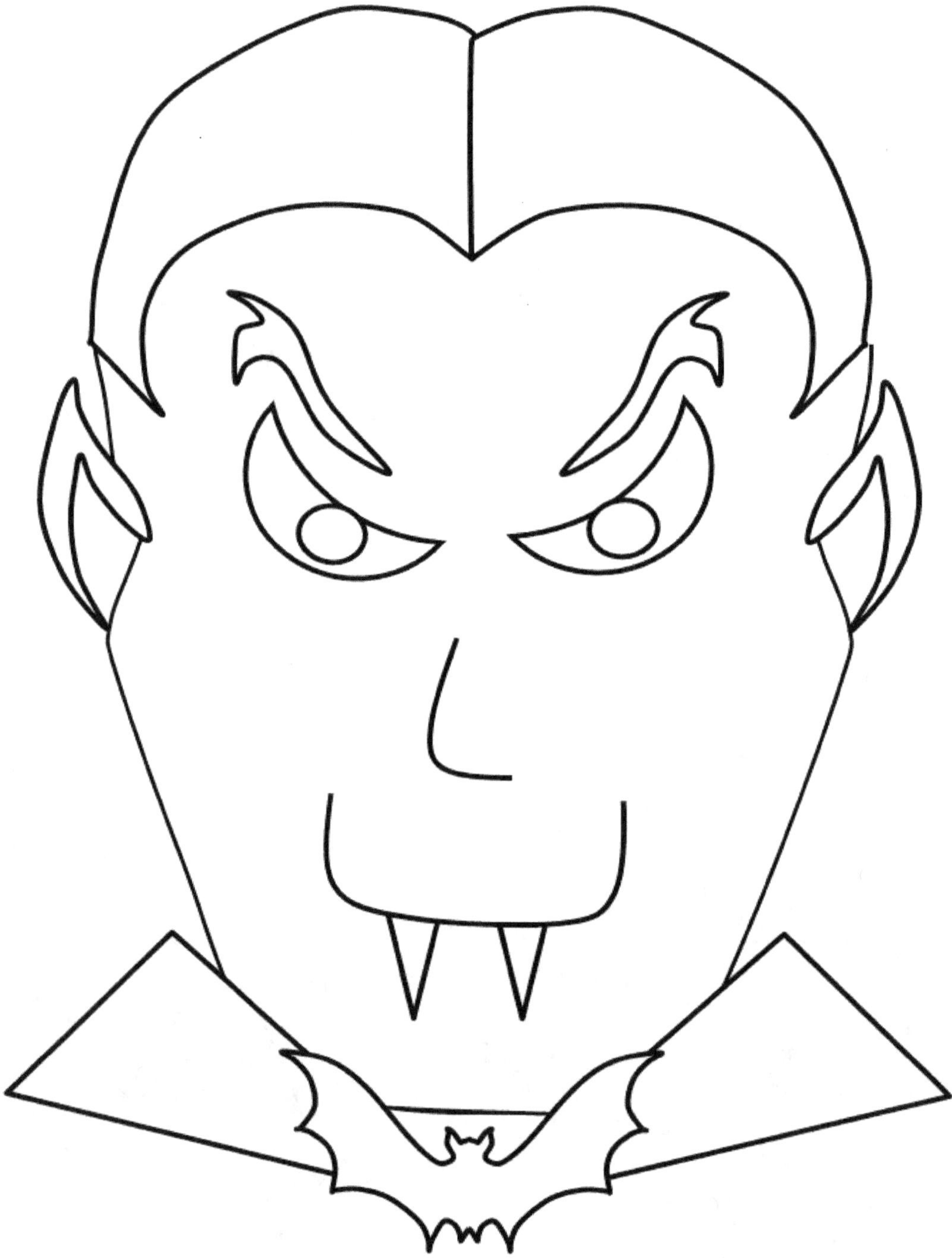

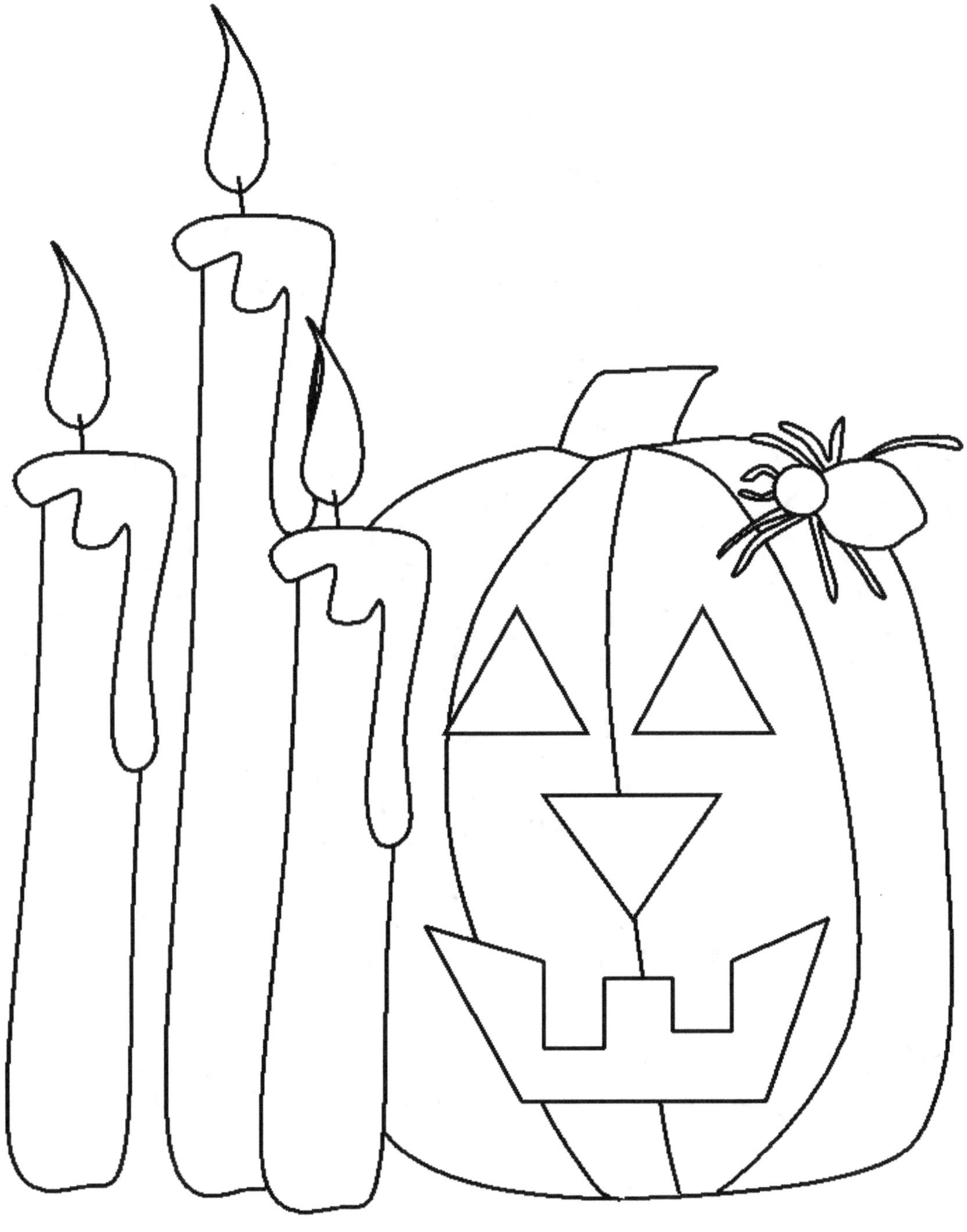

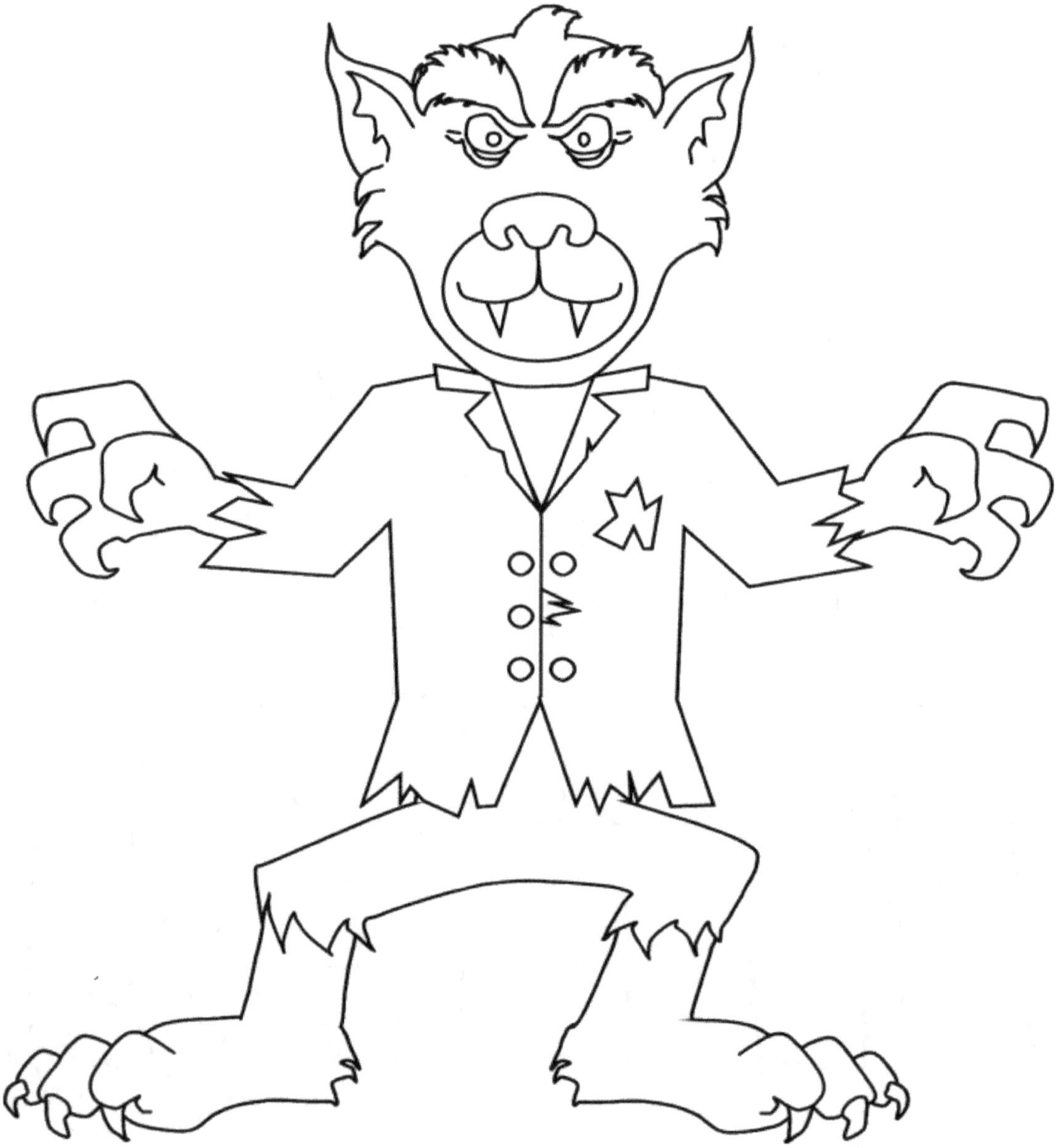

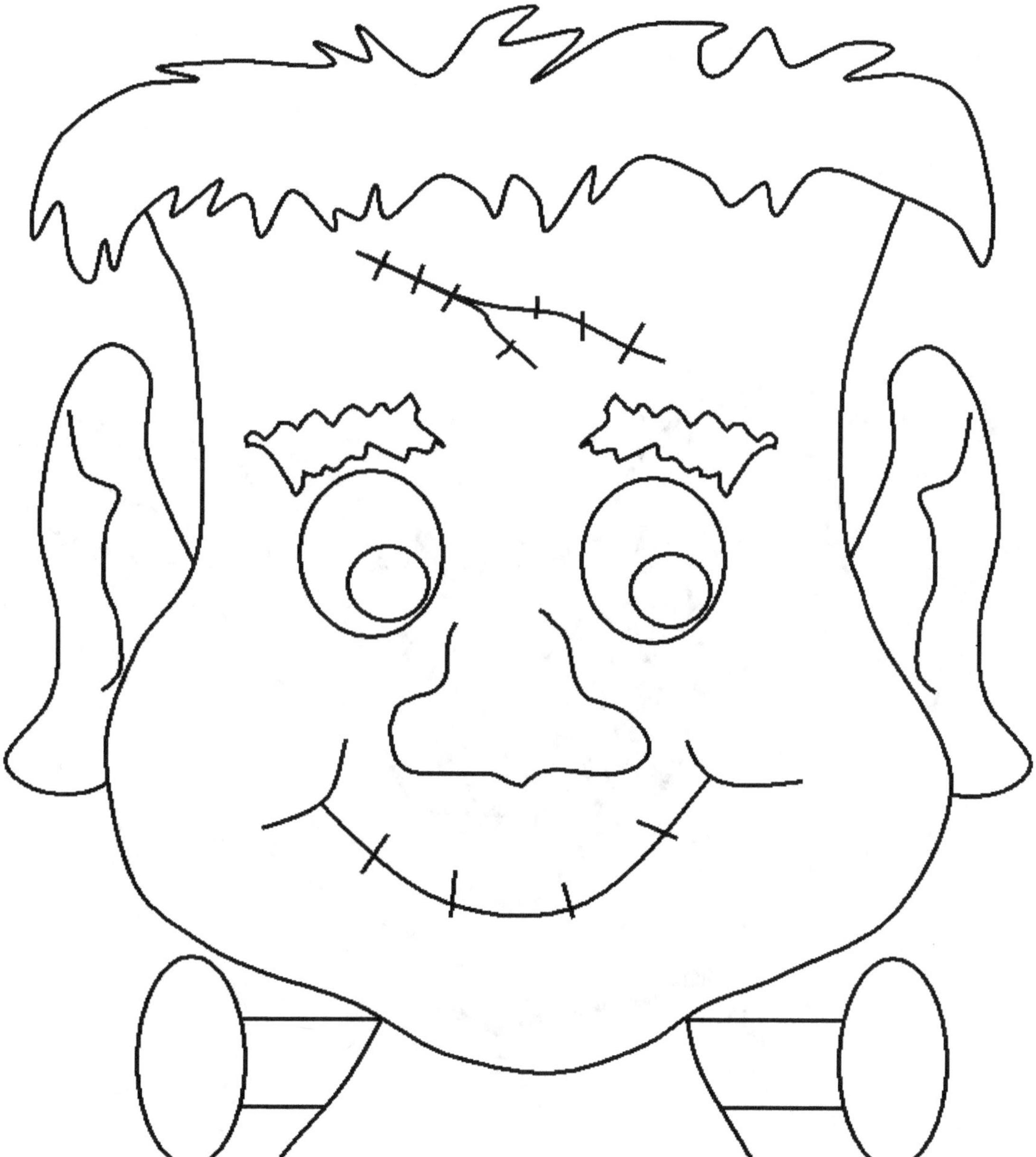

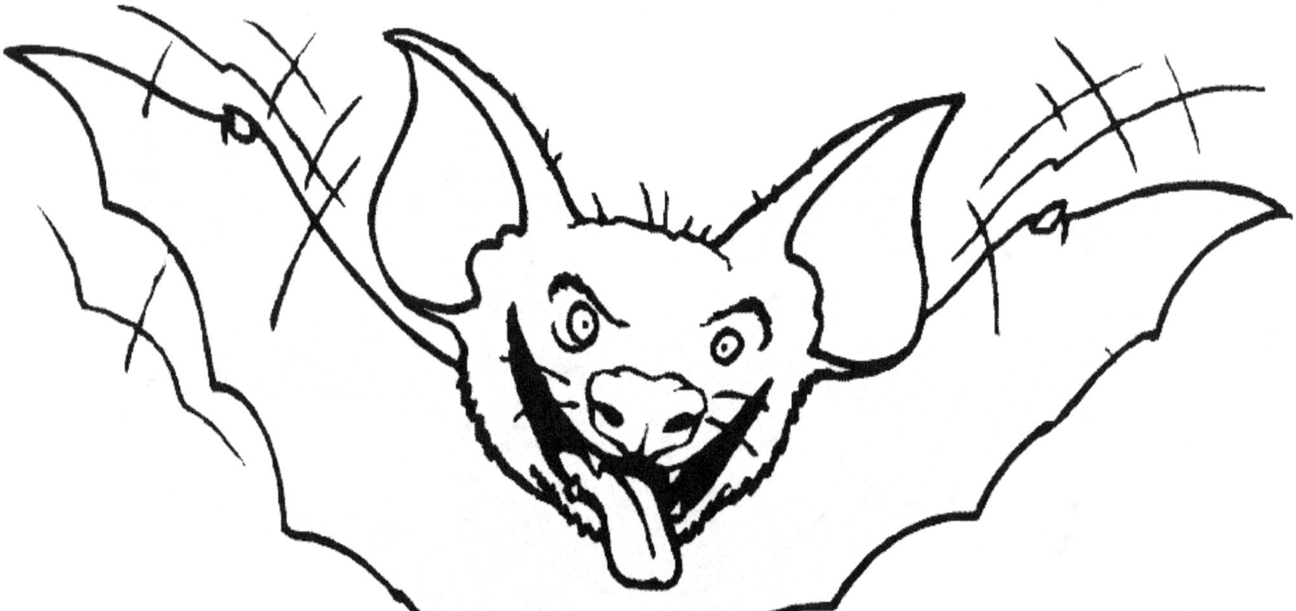

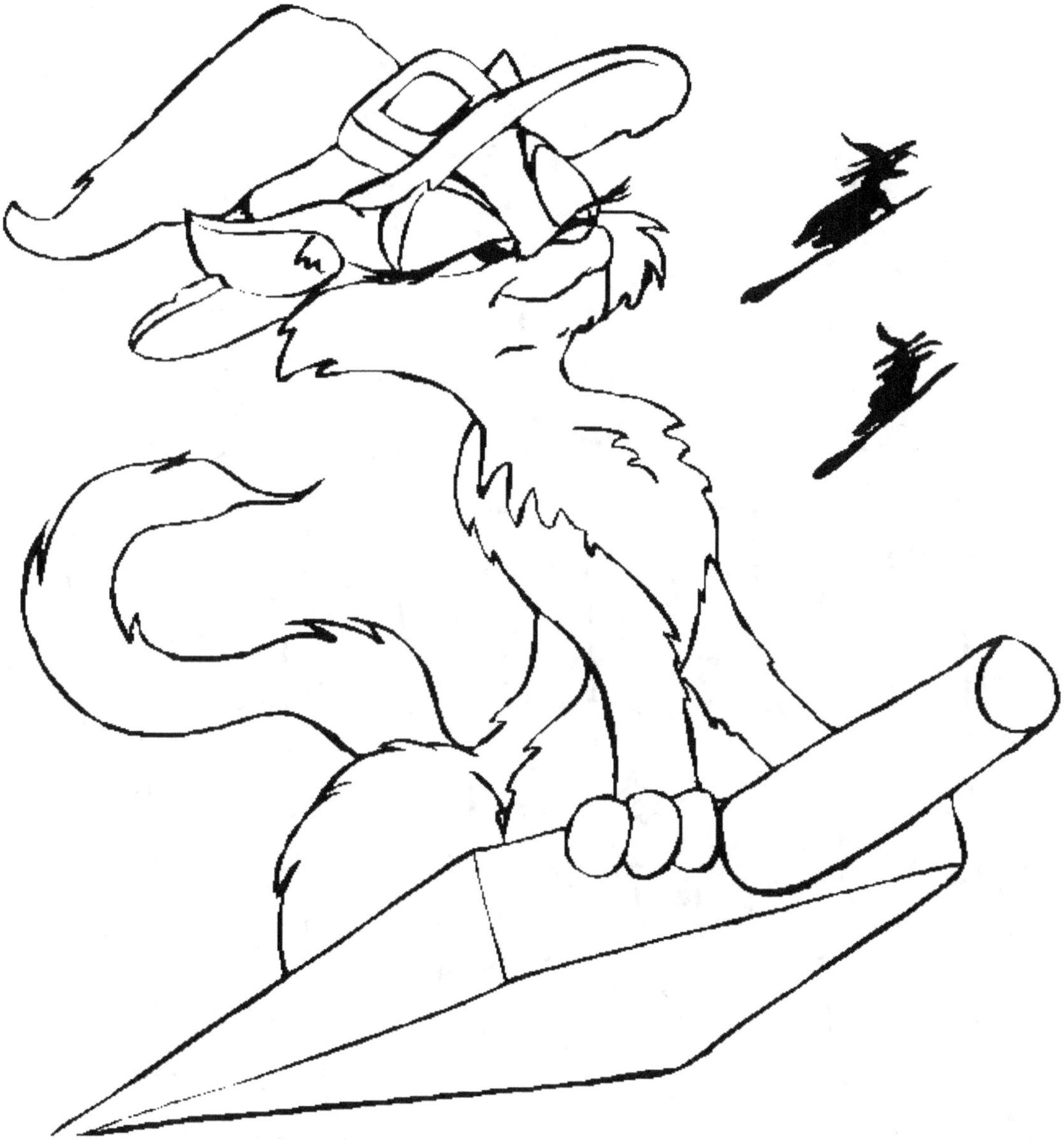

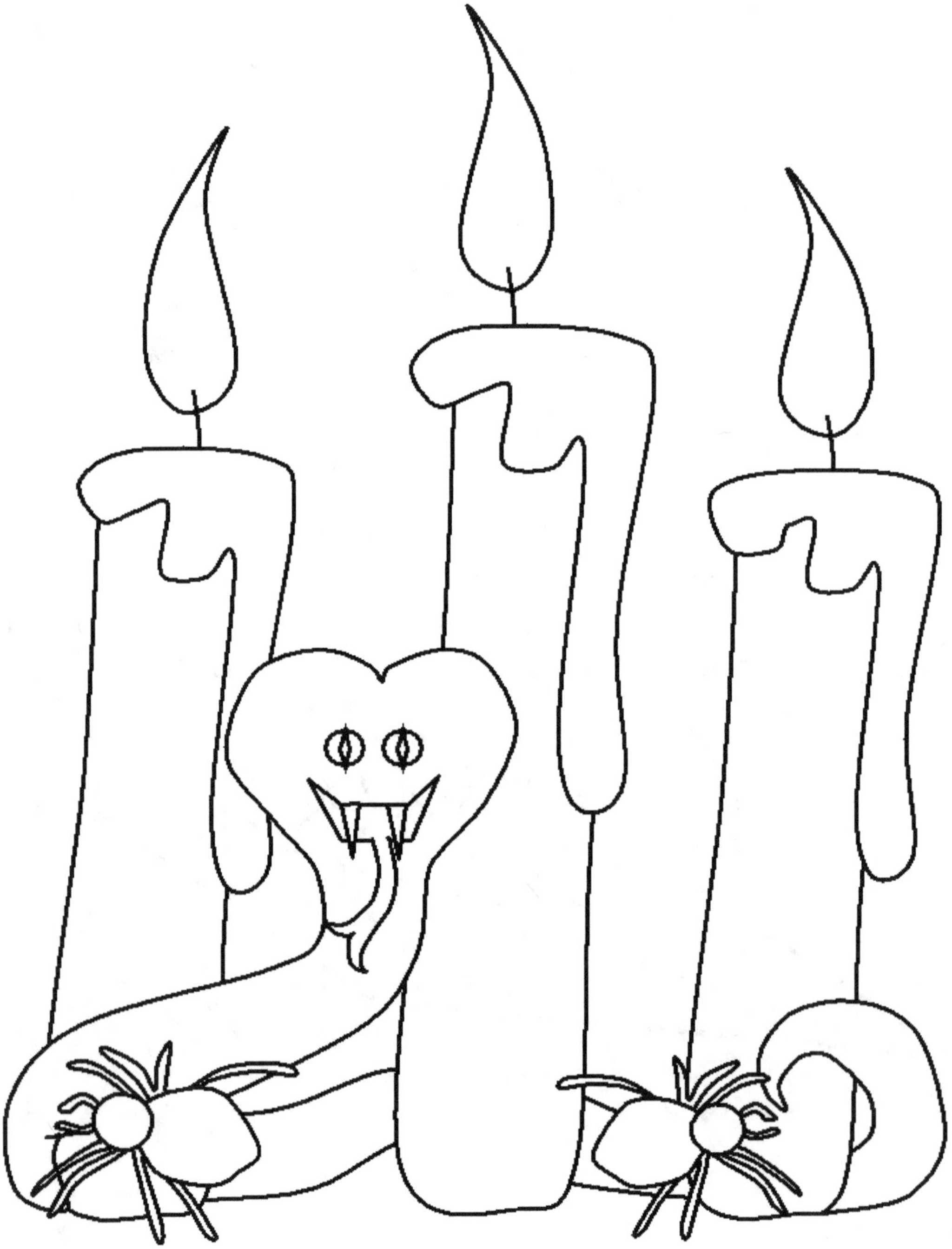

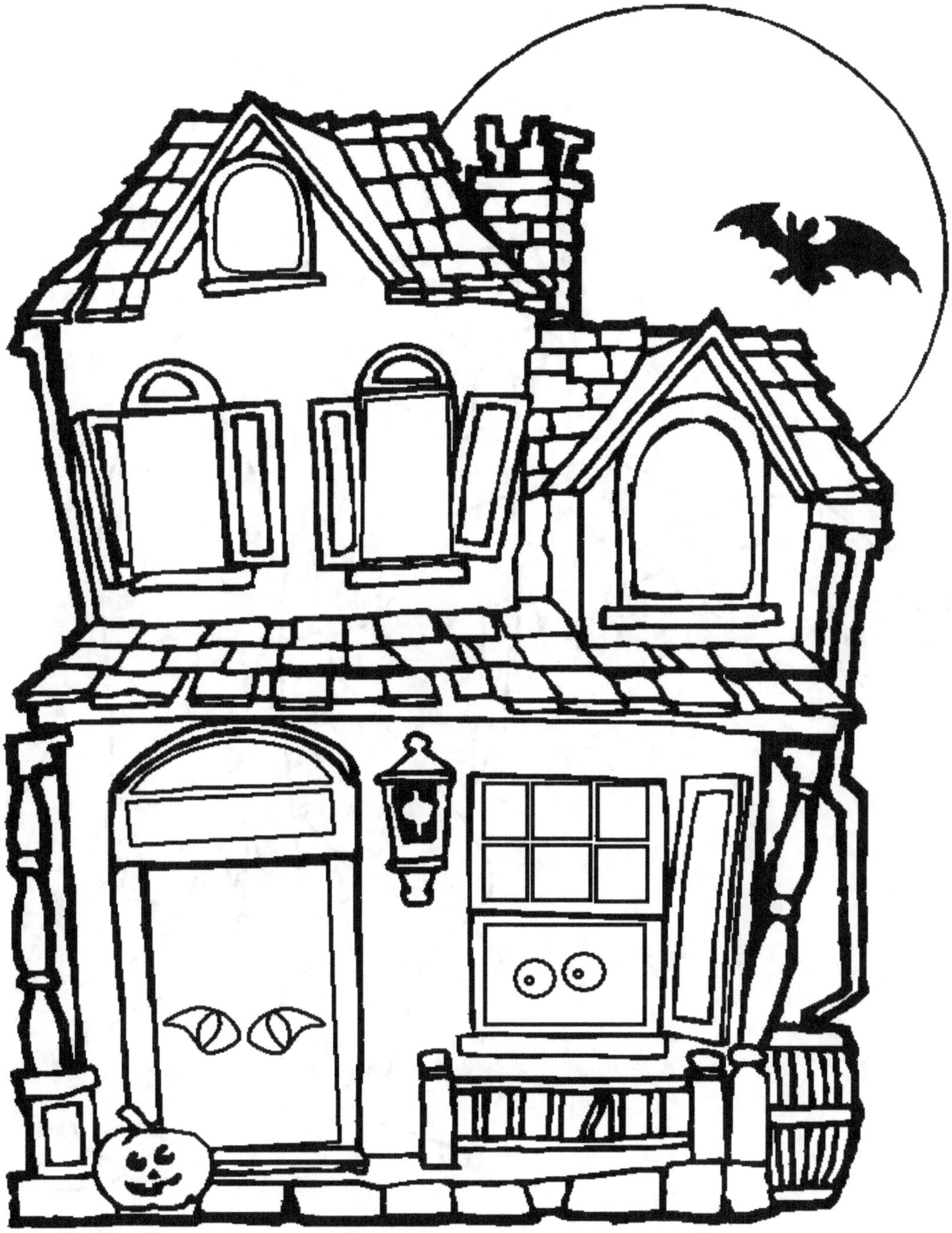

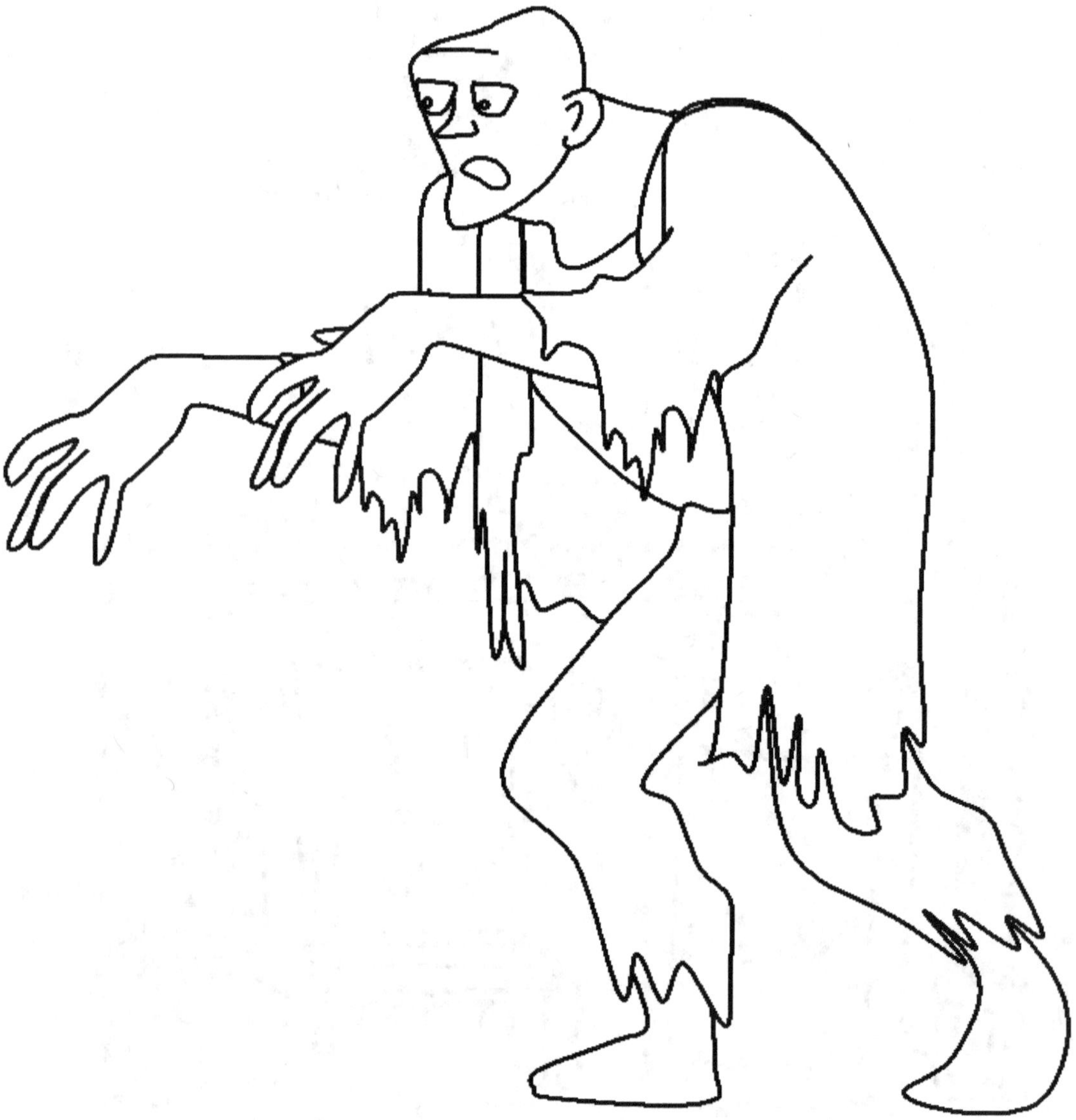

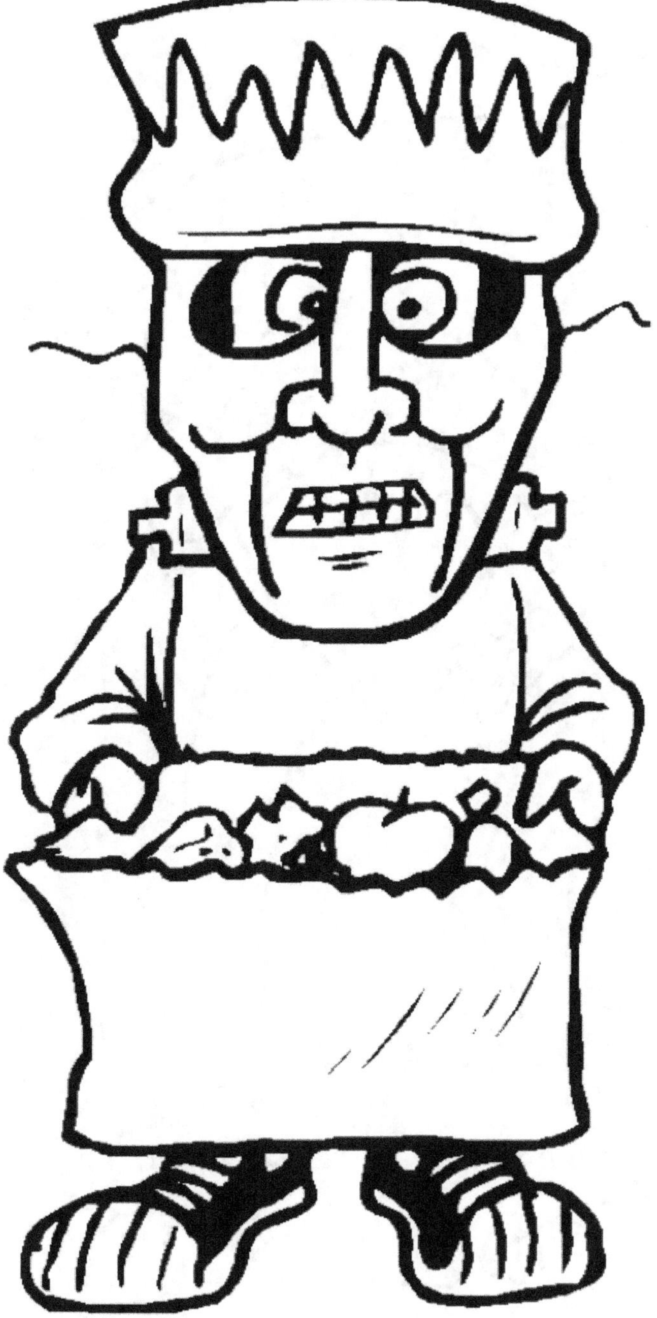

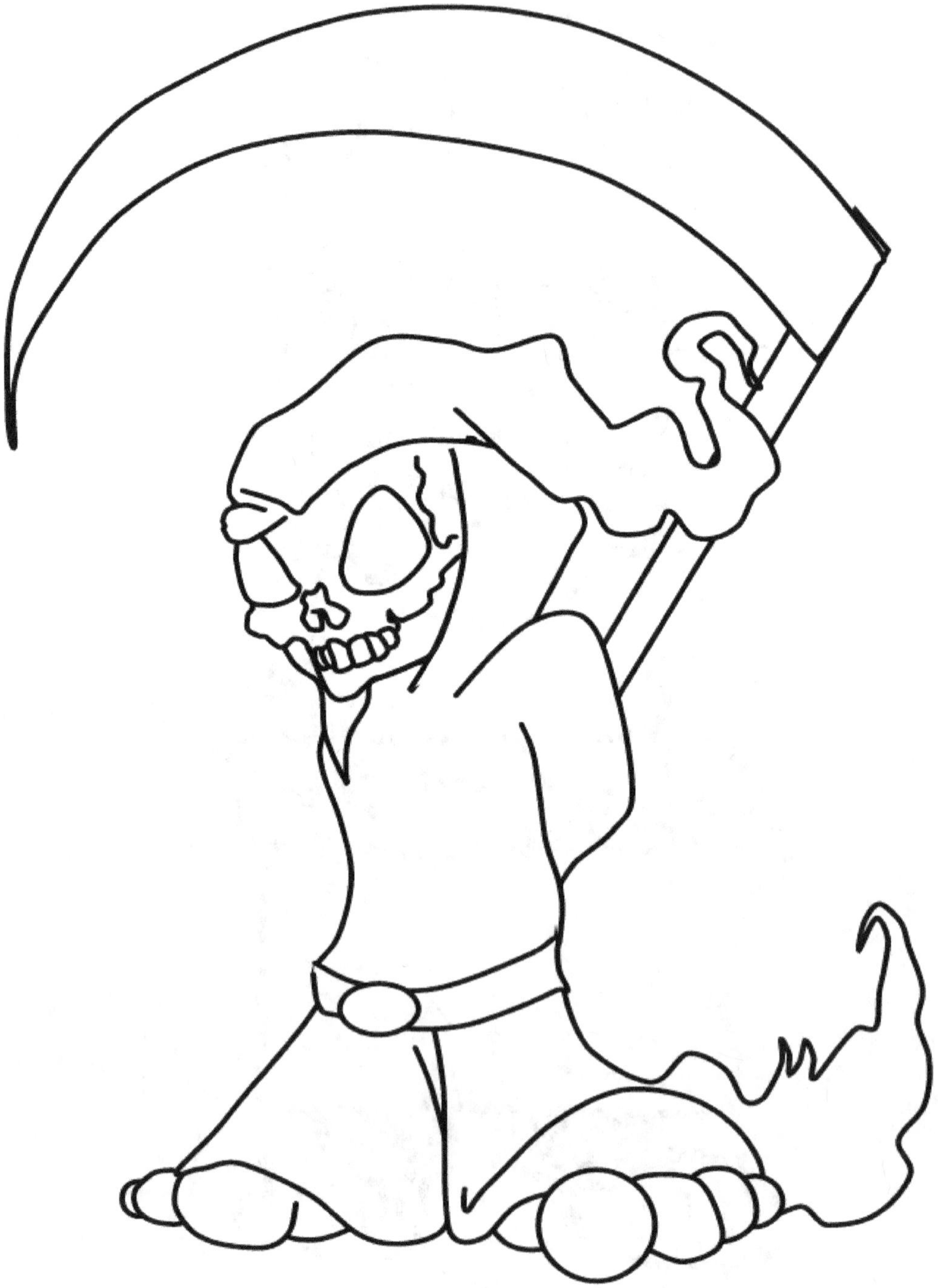

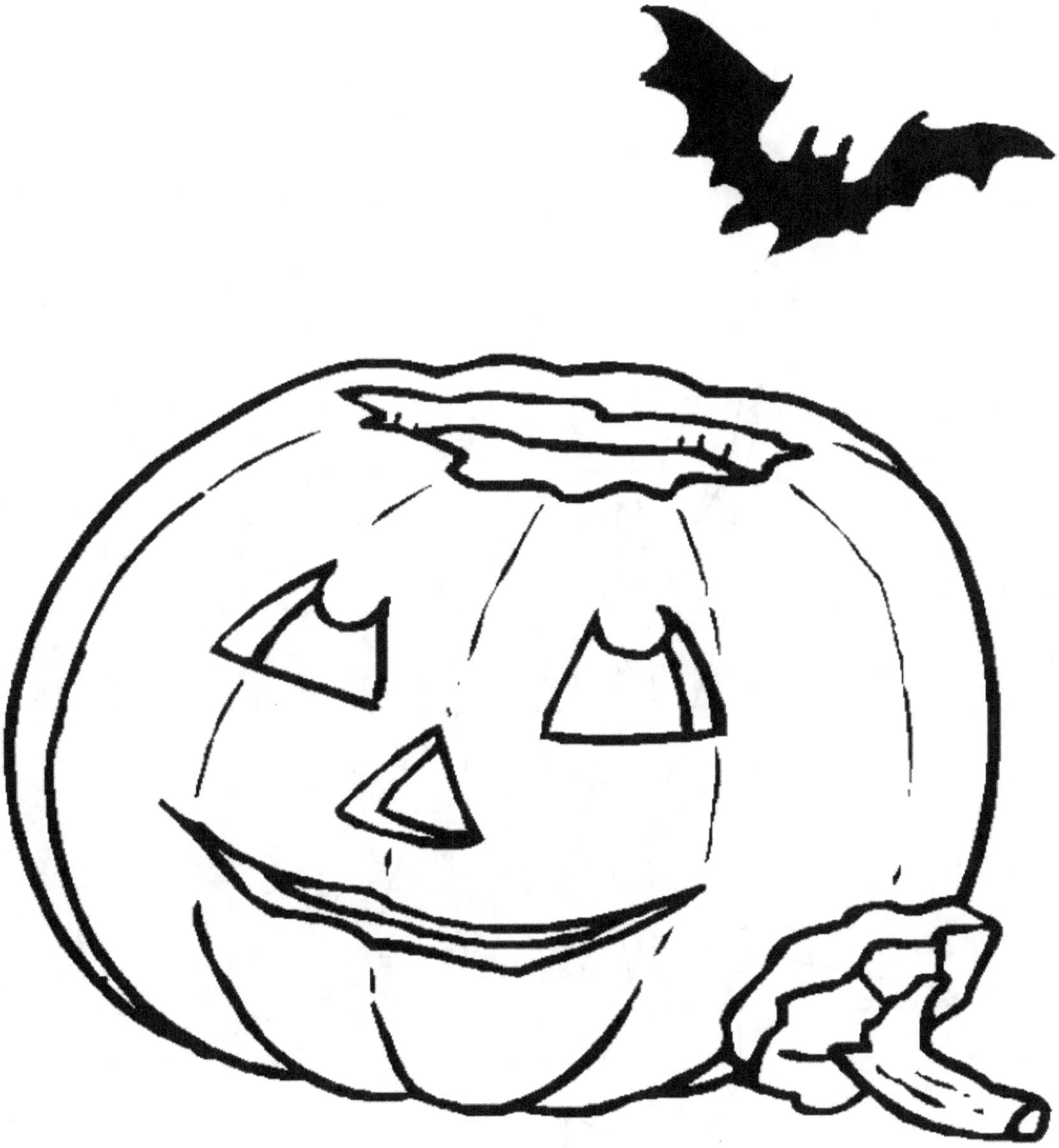

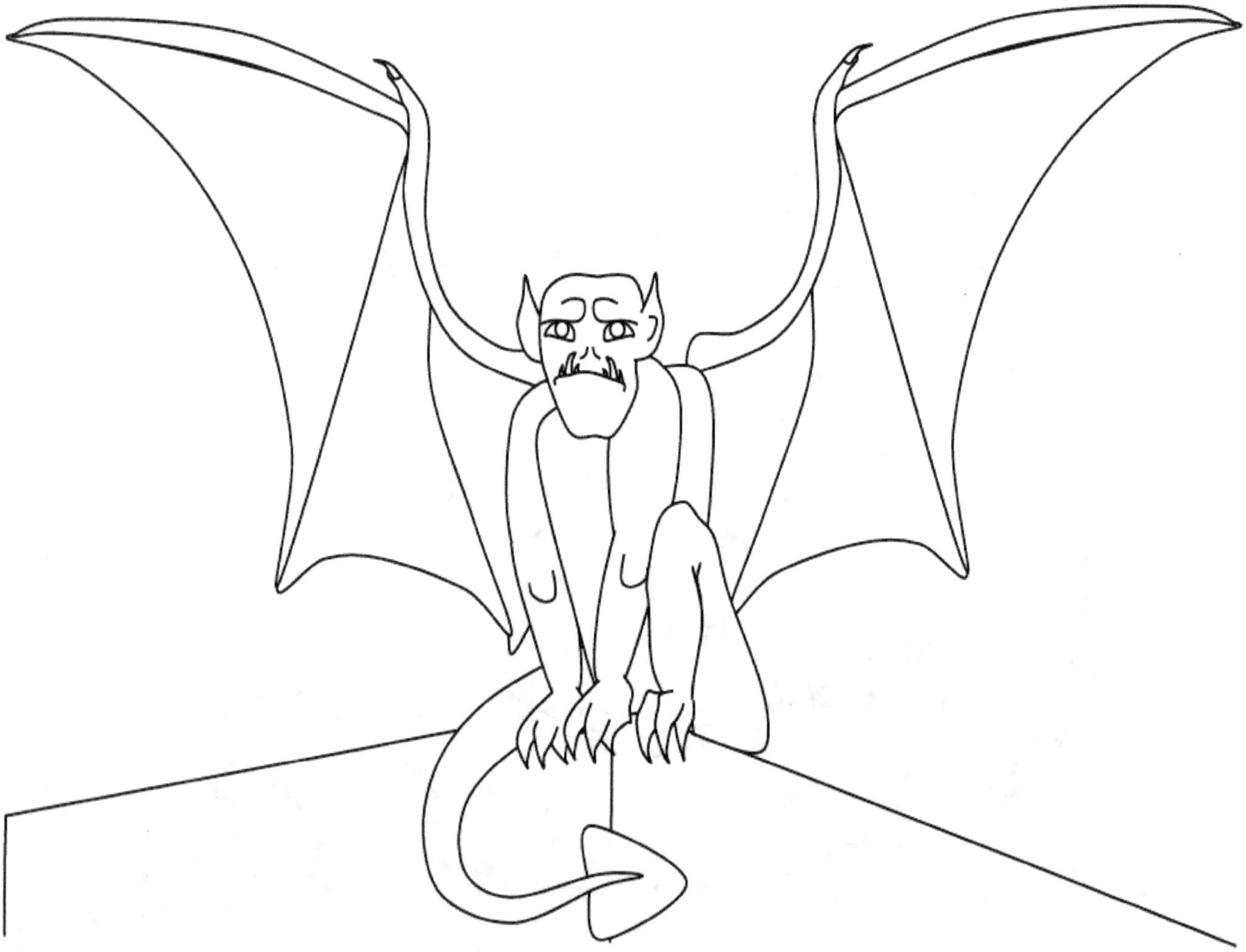

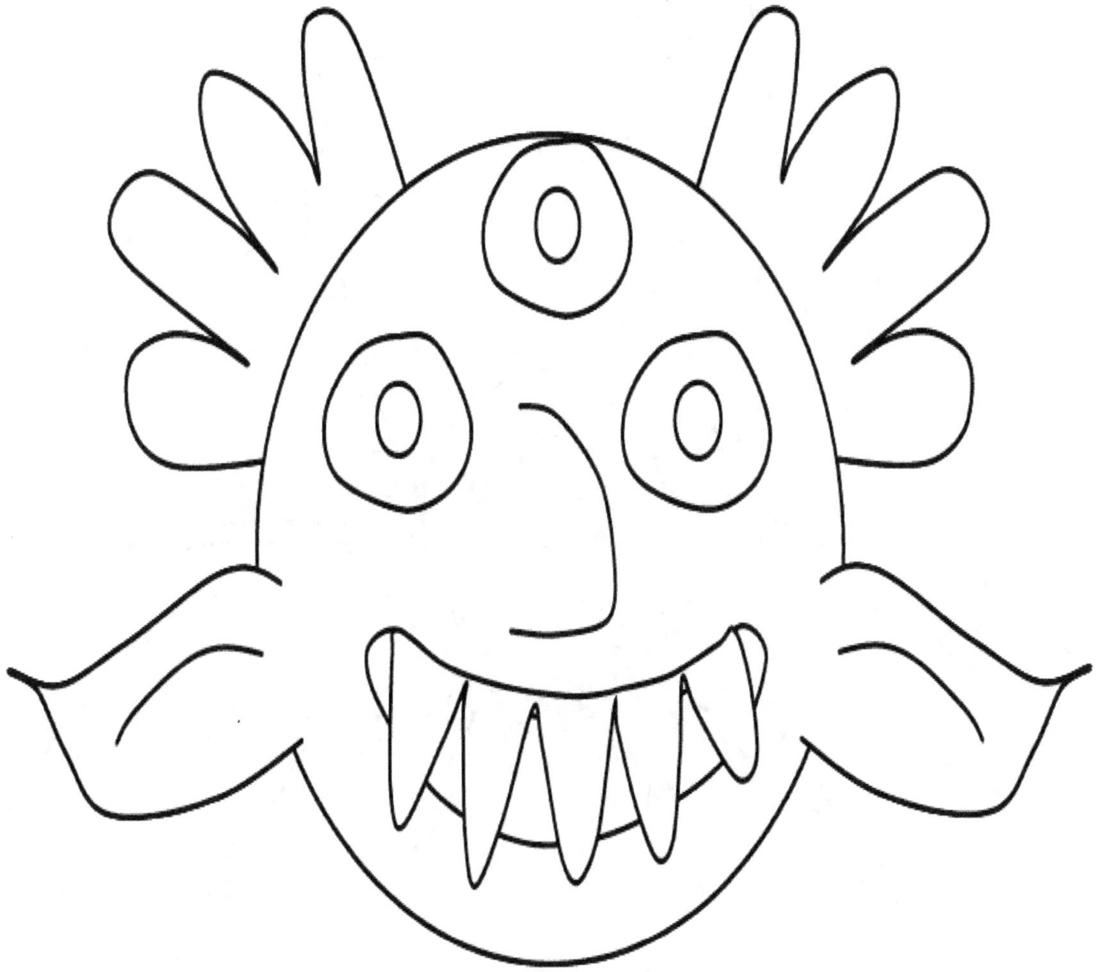

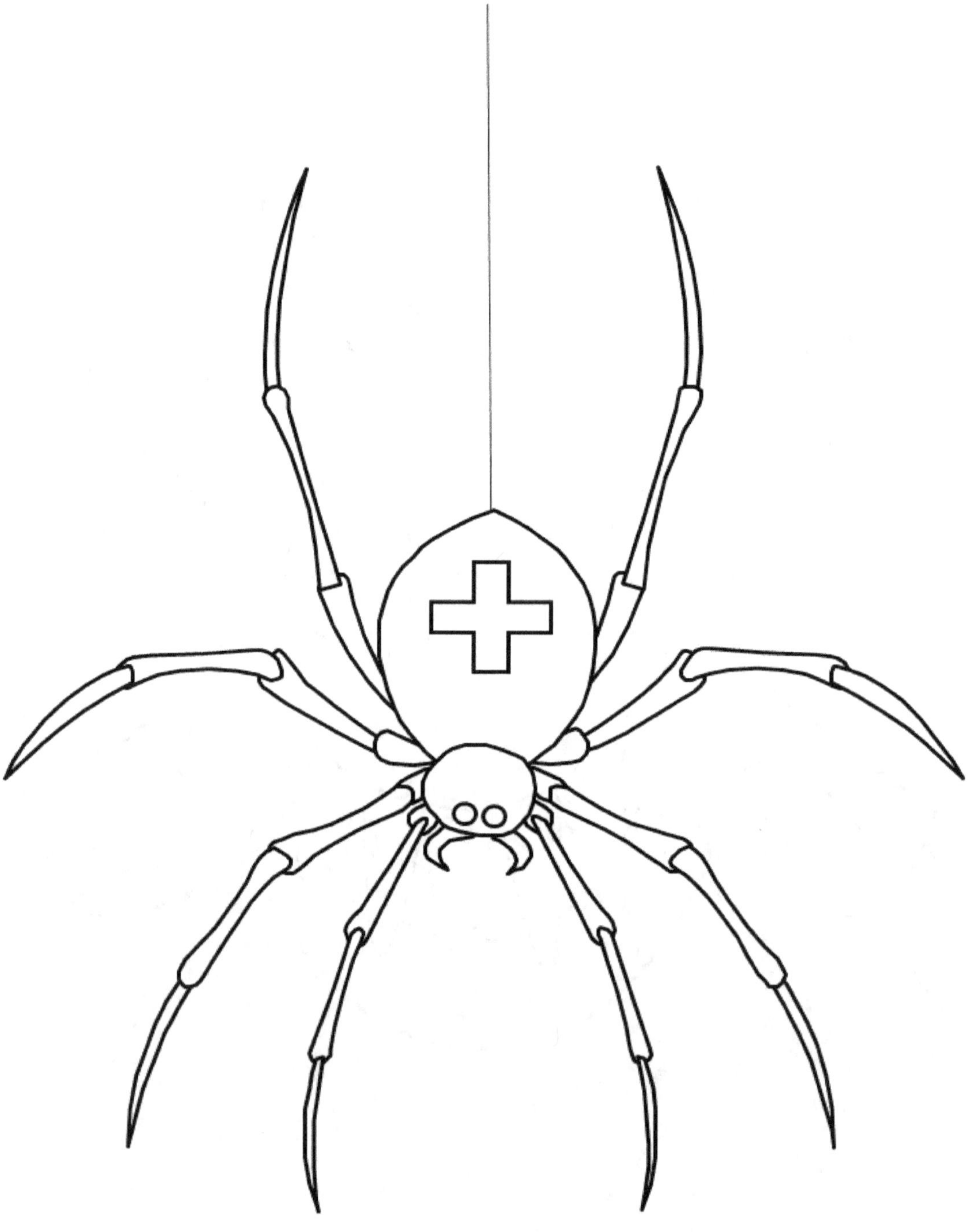

Happy Halloween!

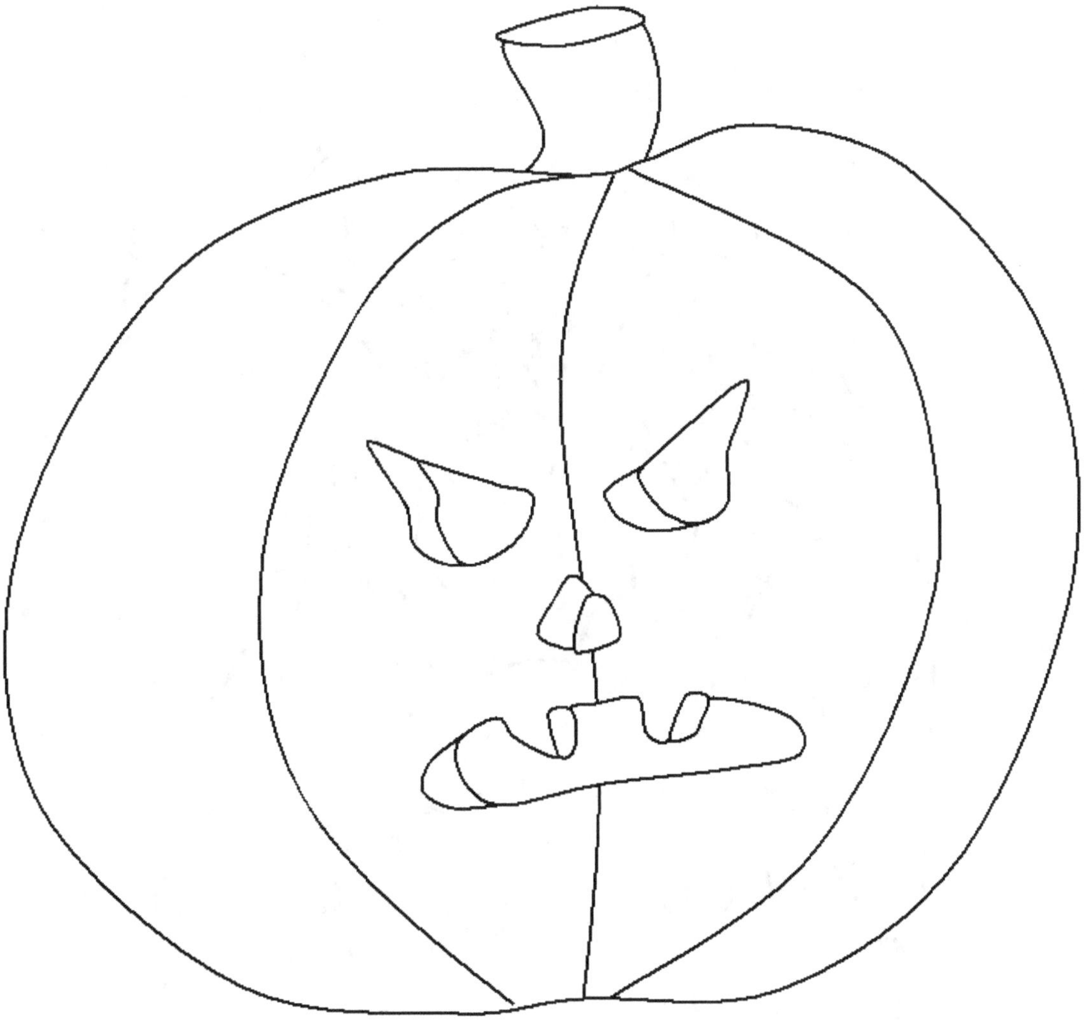

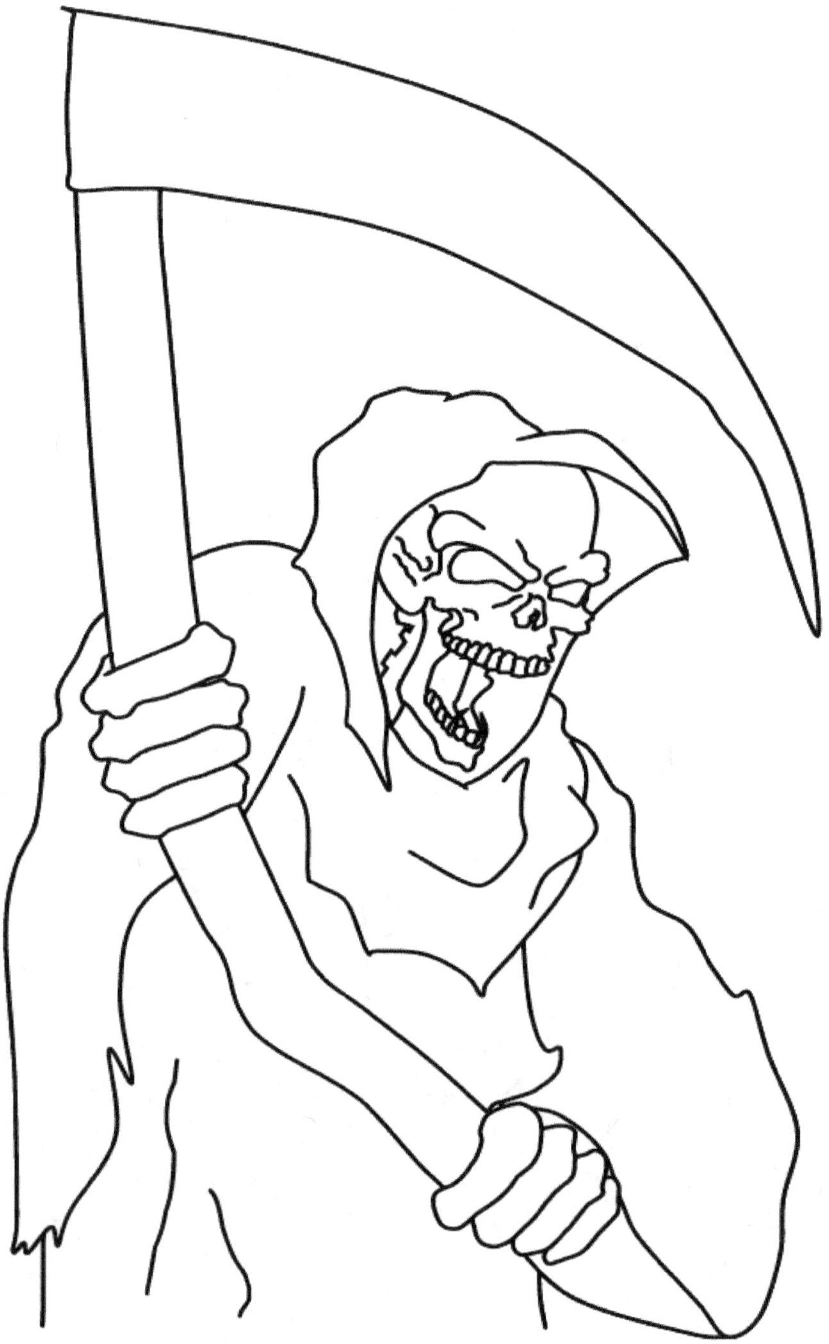

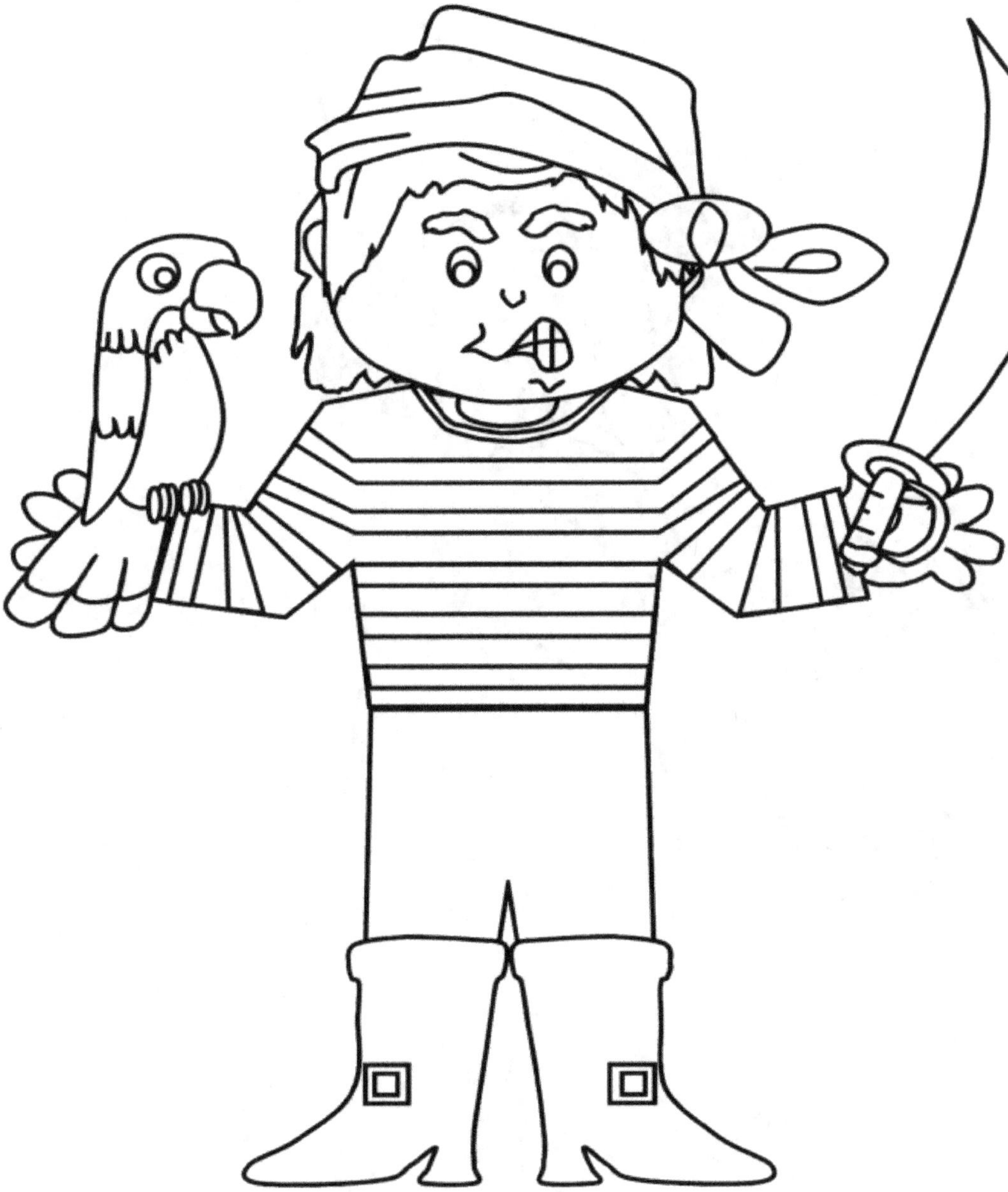

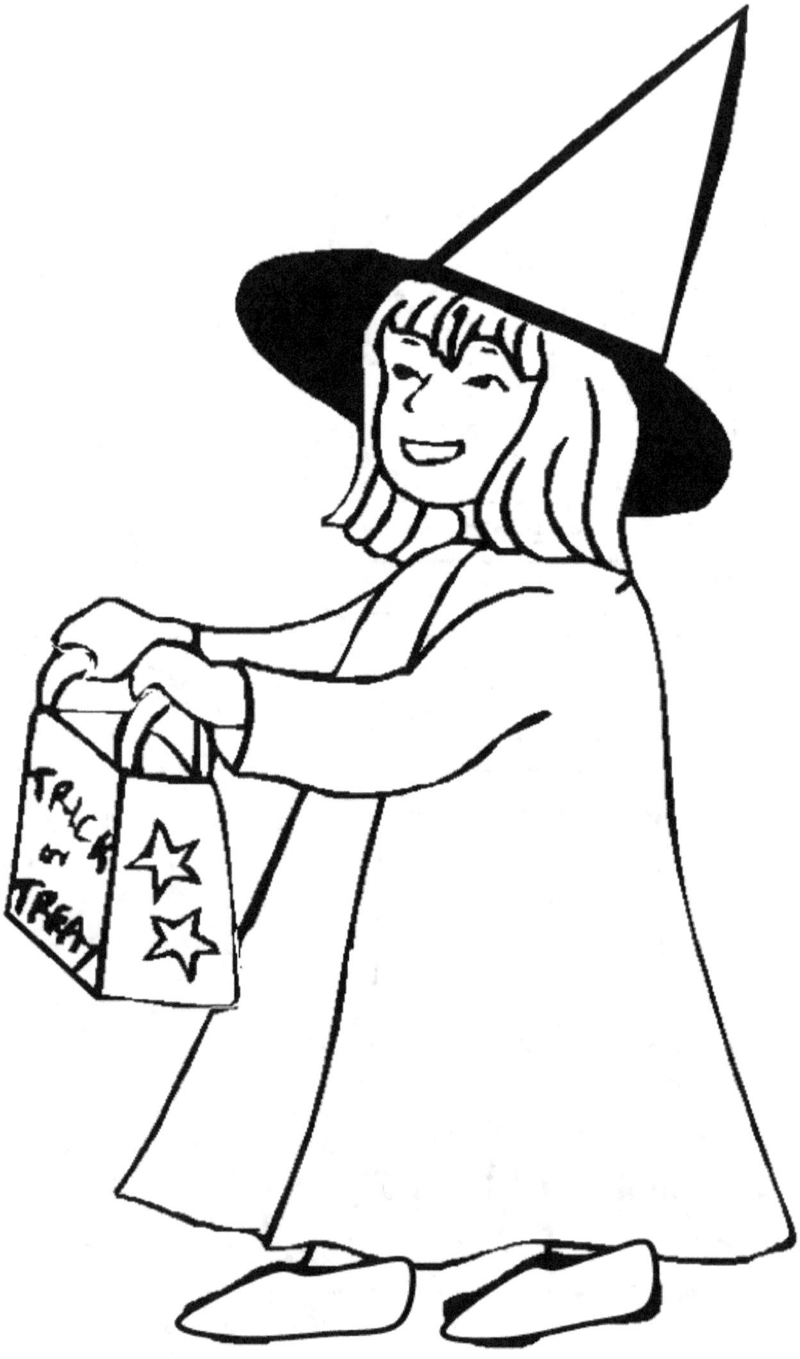
TRICK
or
TREAT

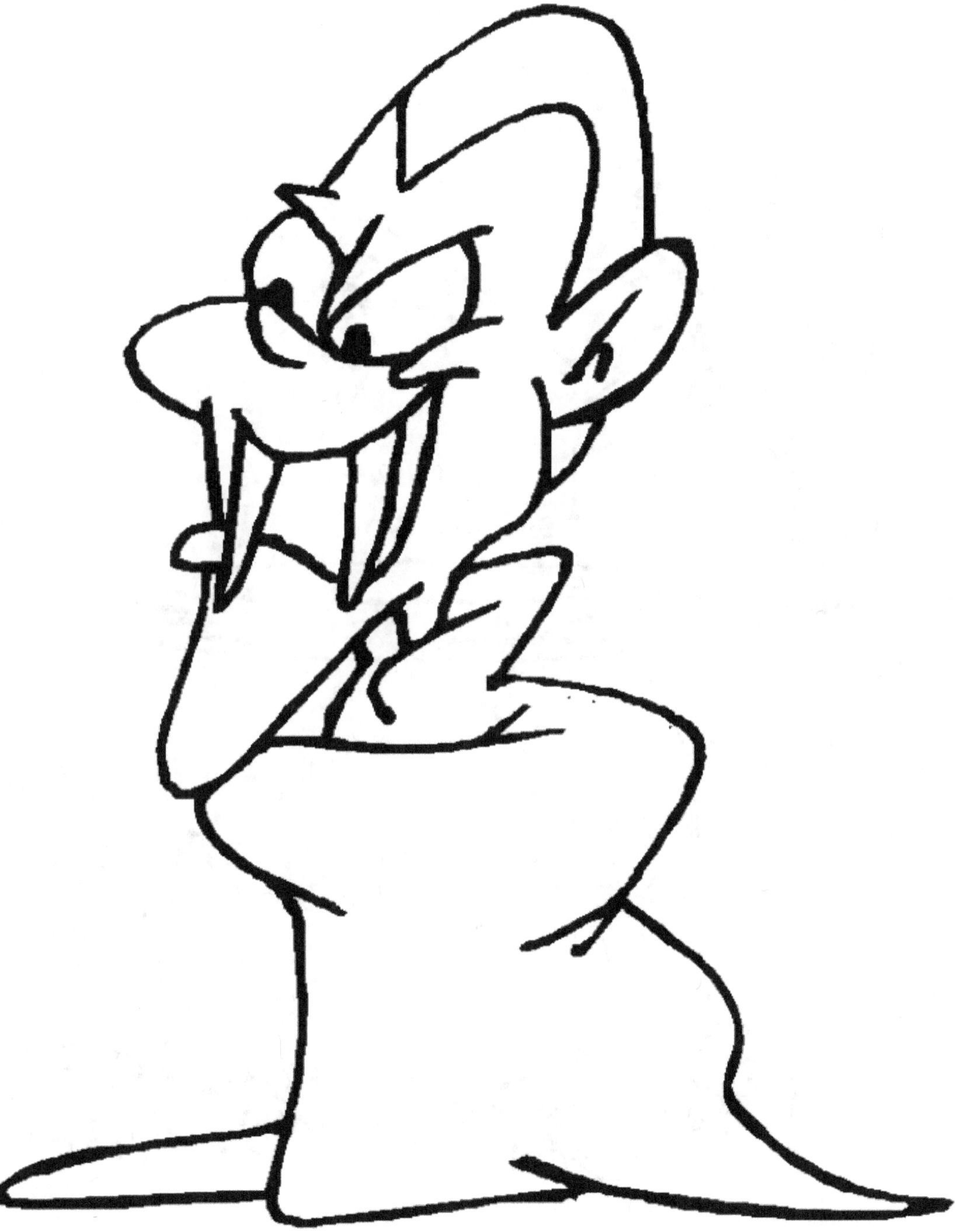

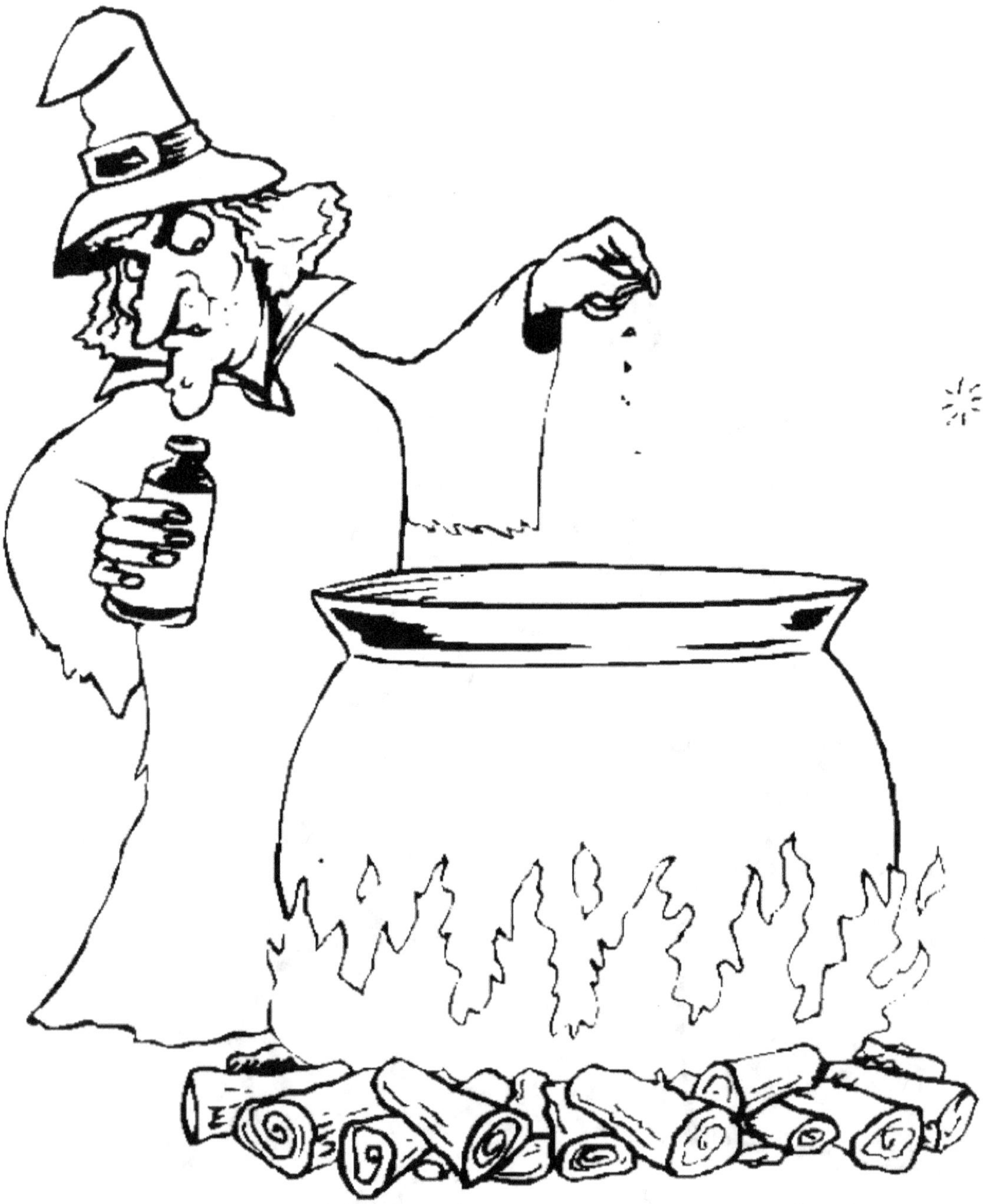

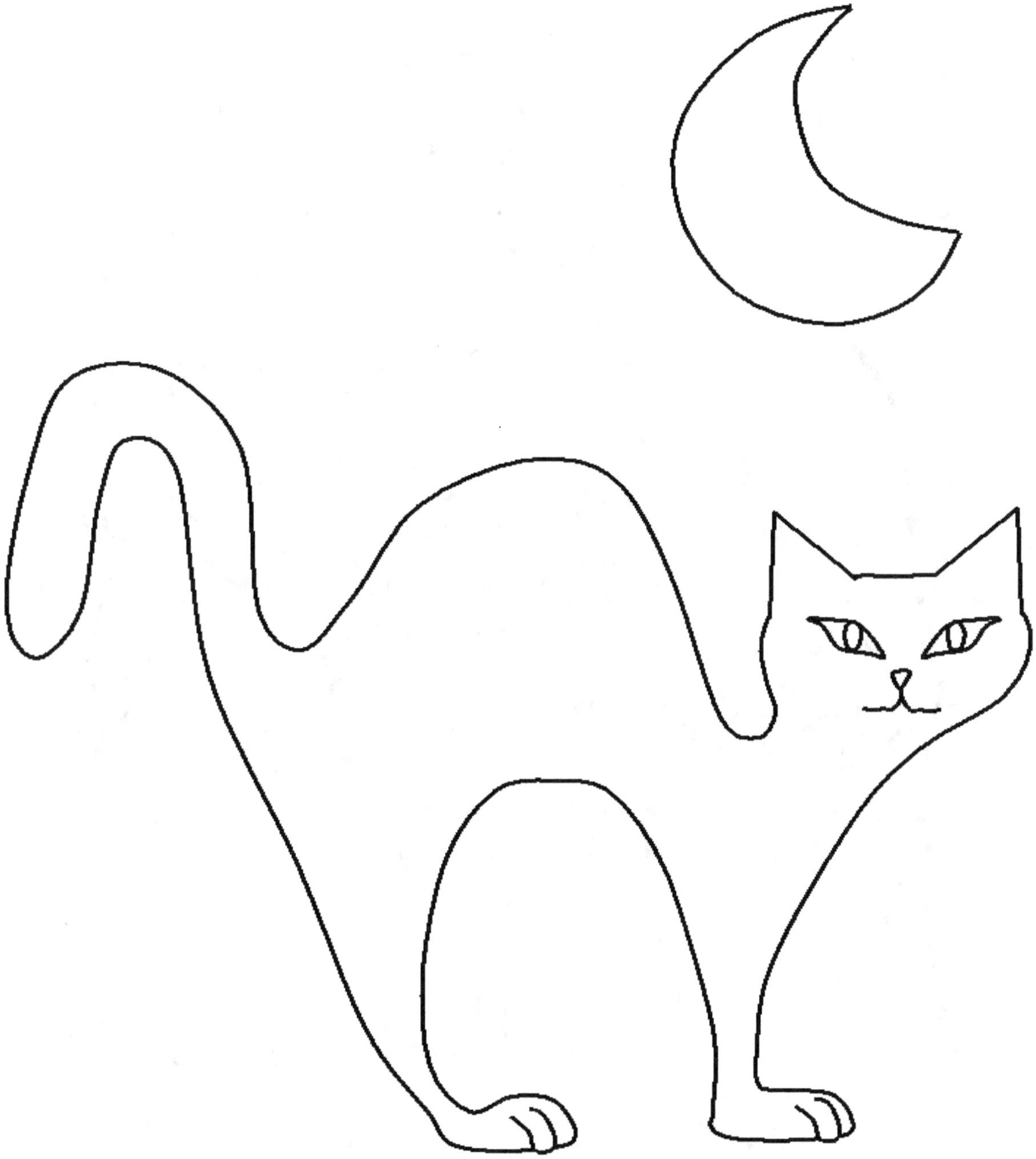

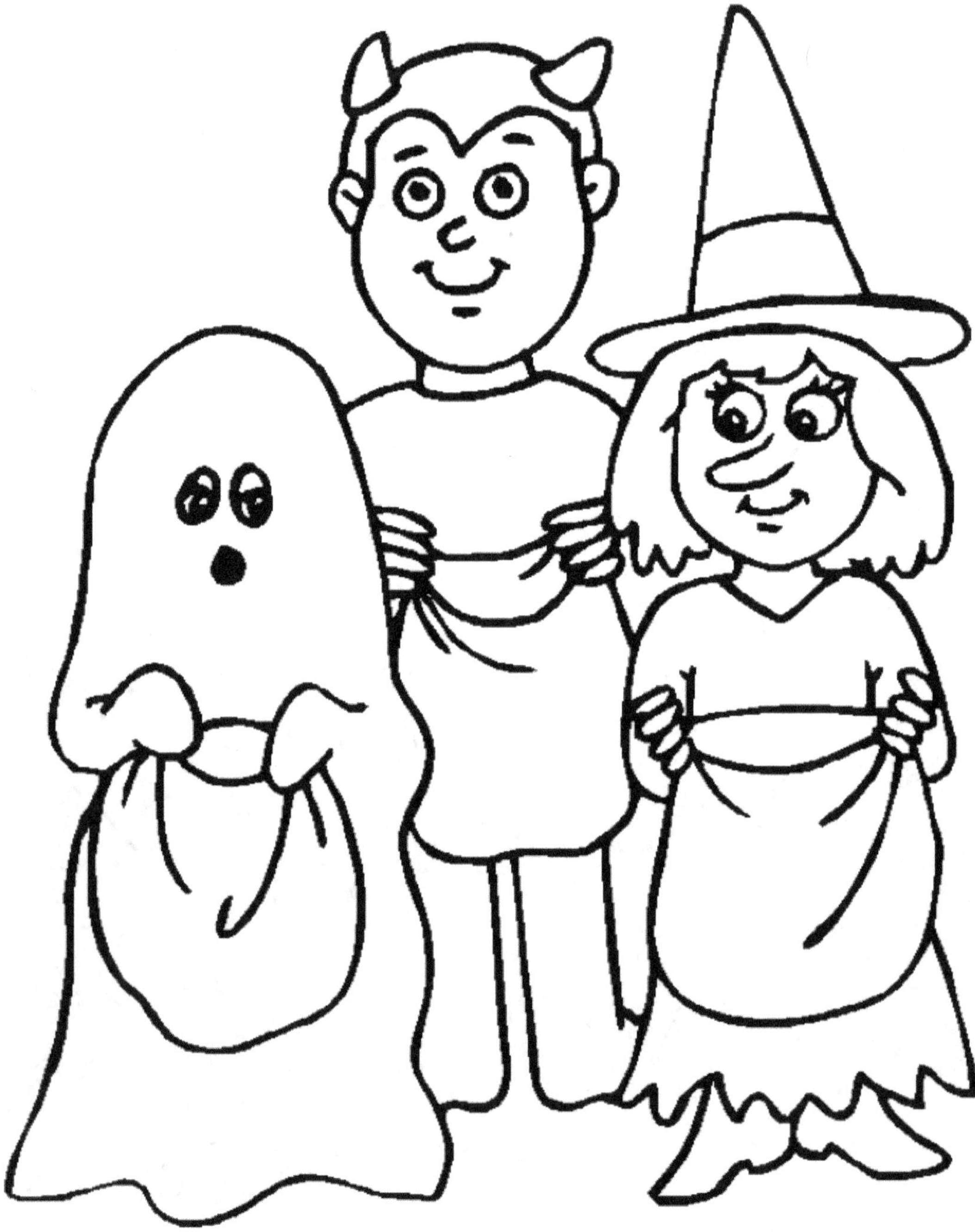

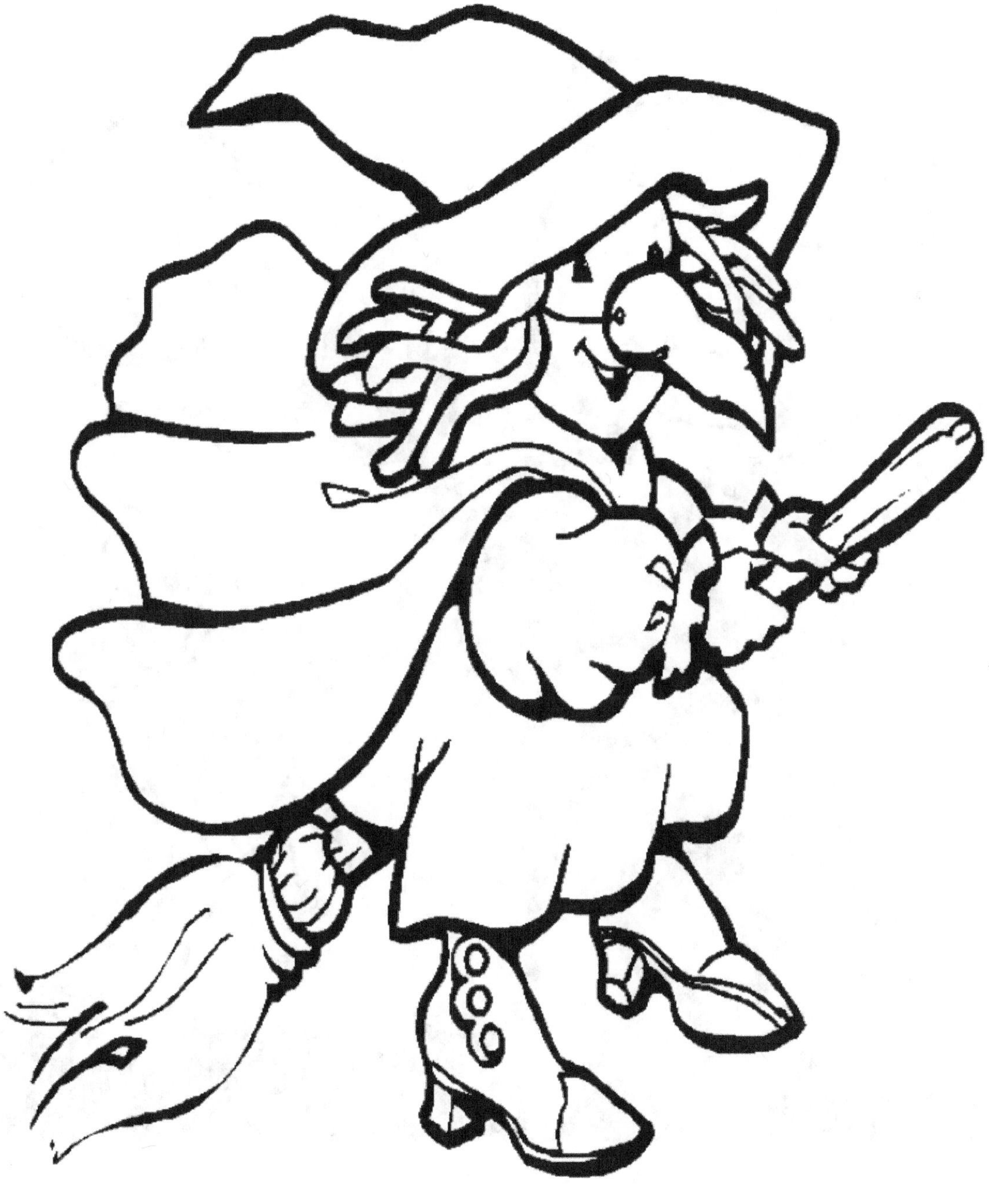

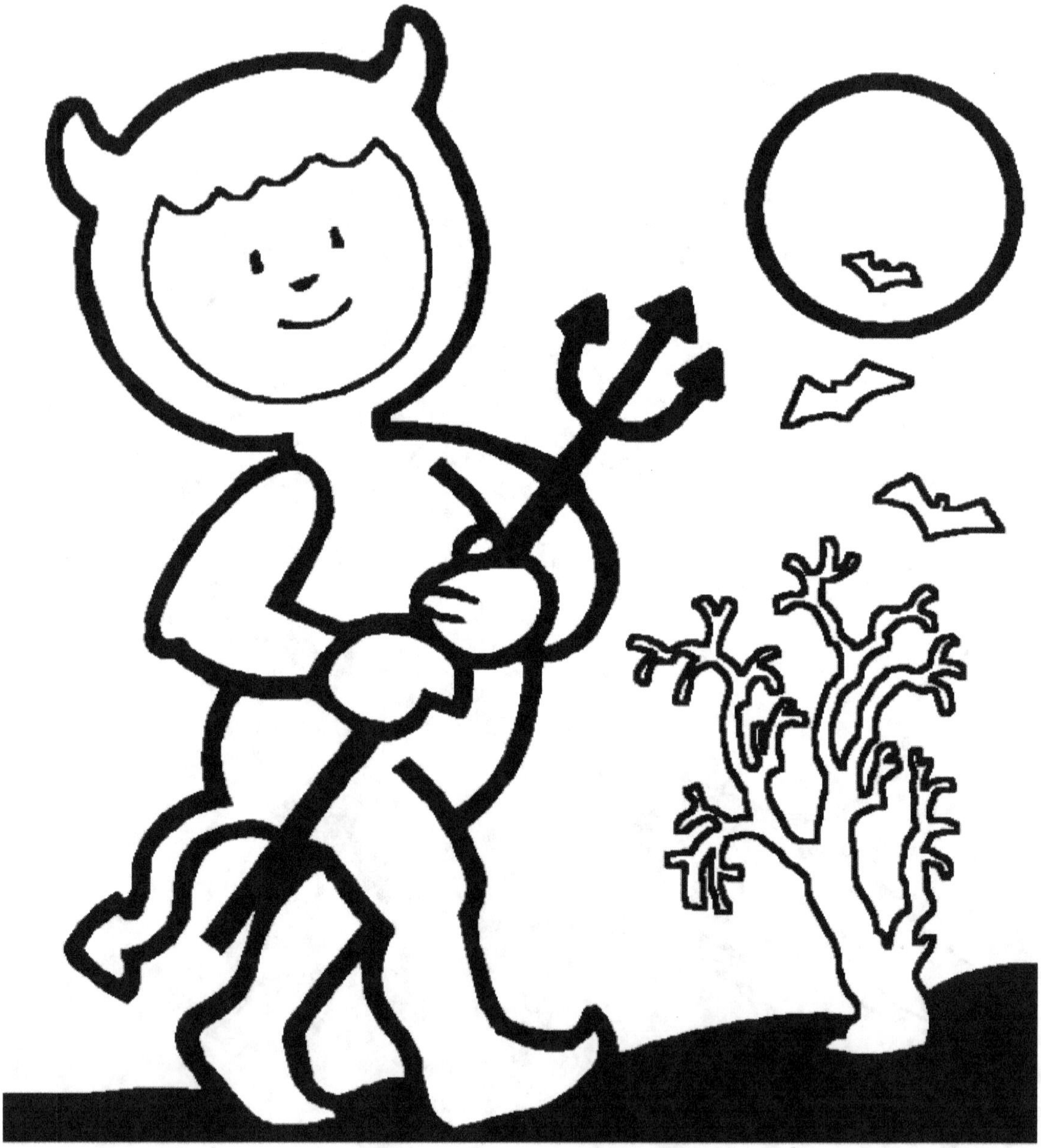

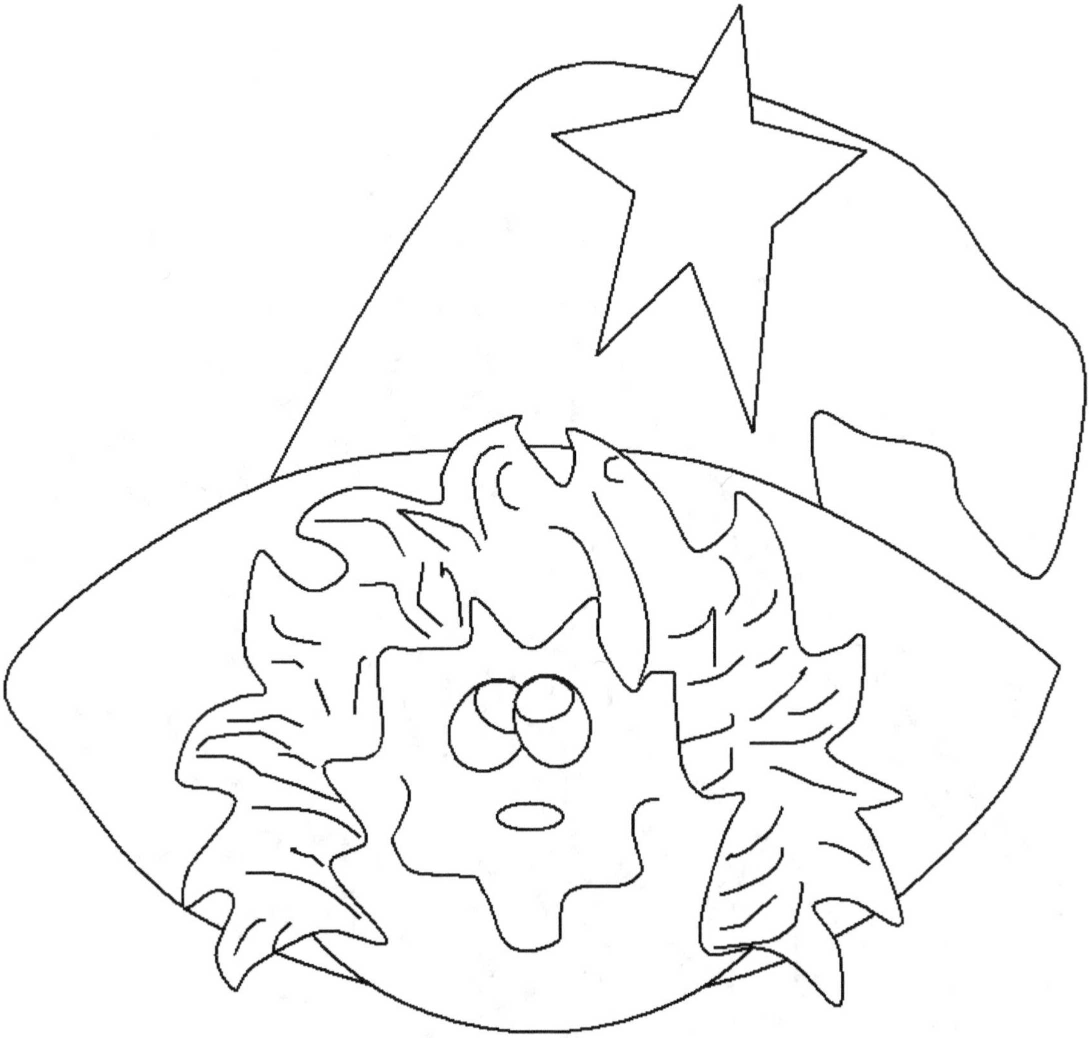

Happy
Halloween!

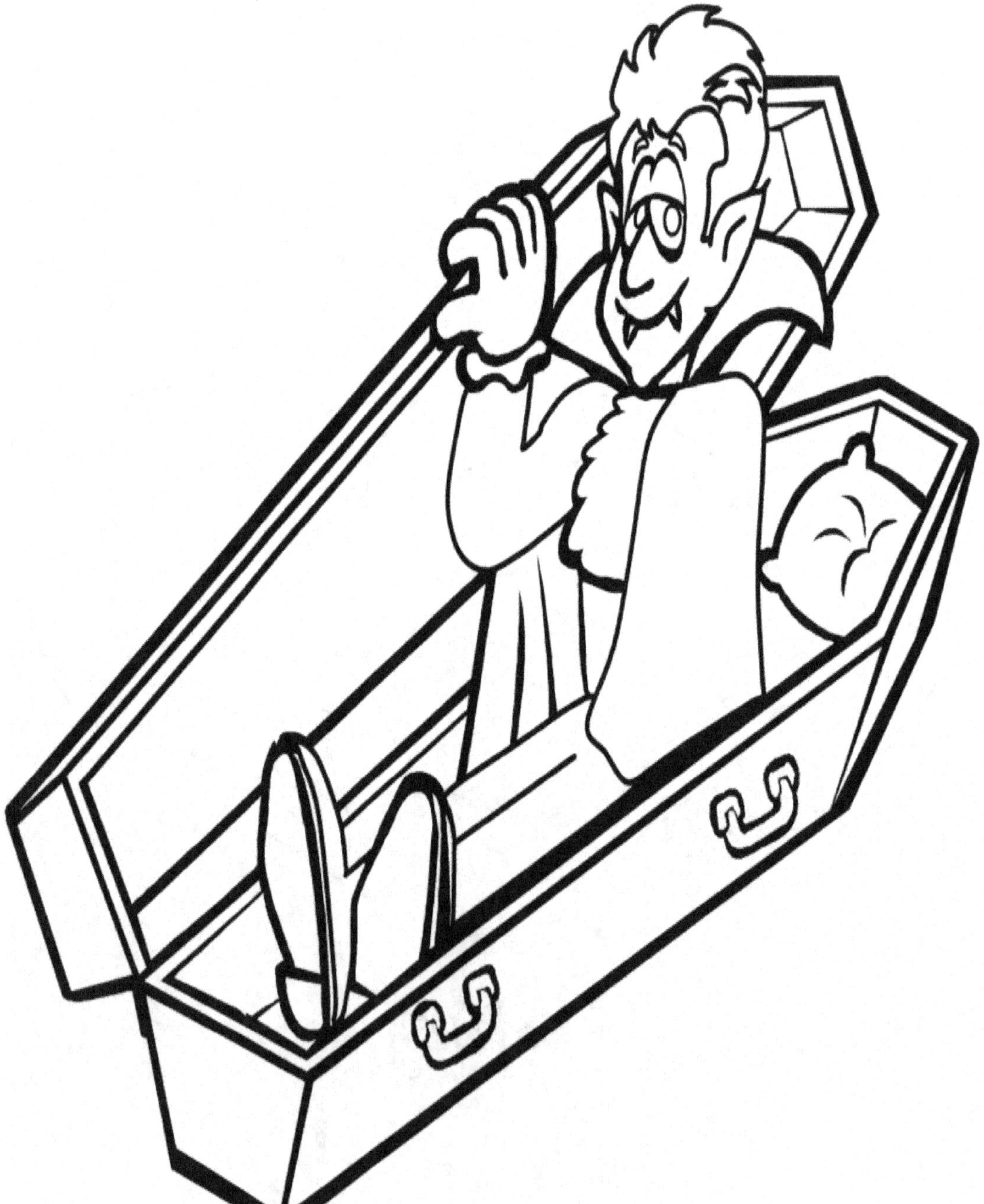

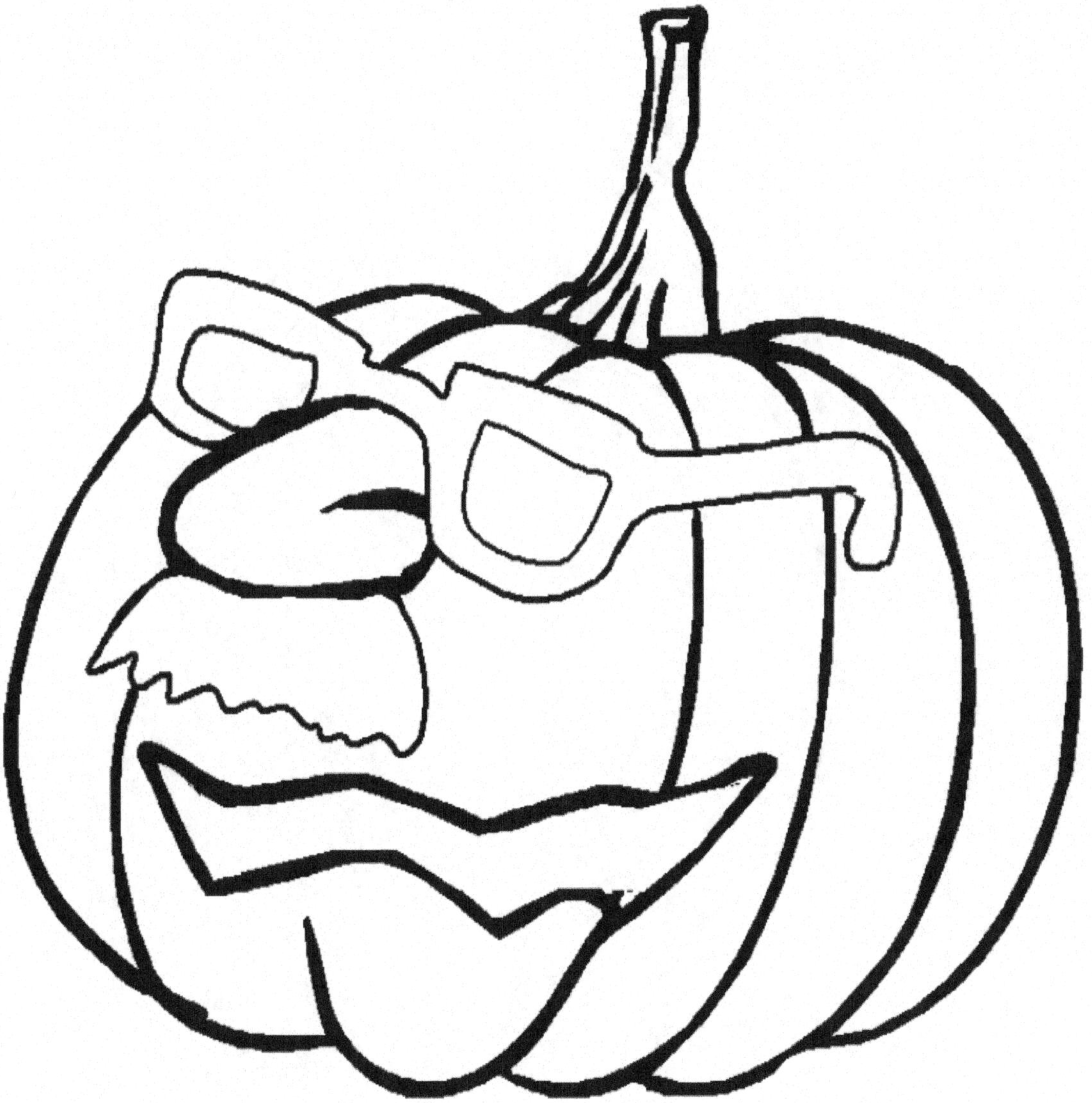

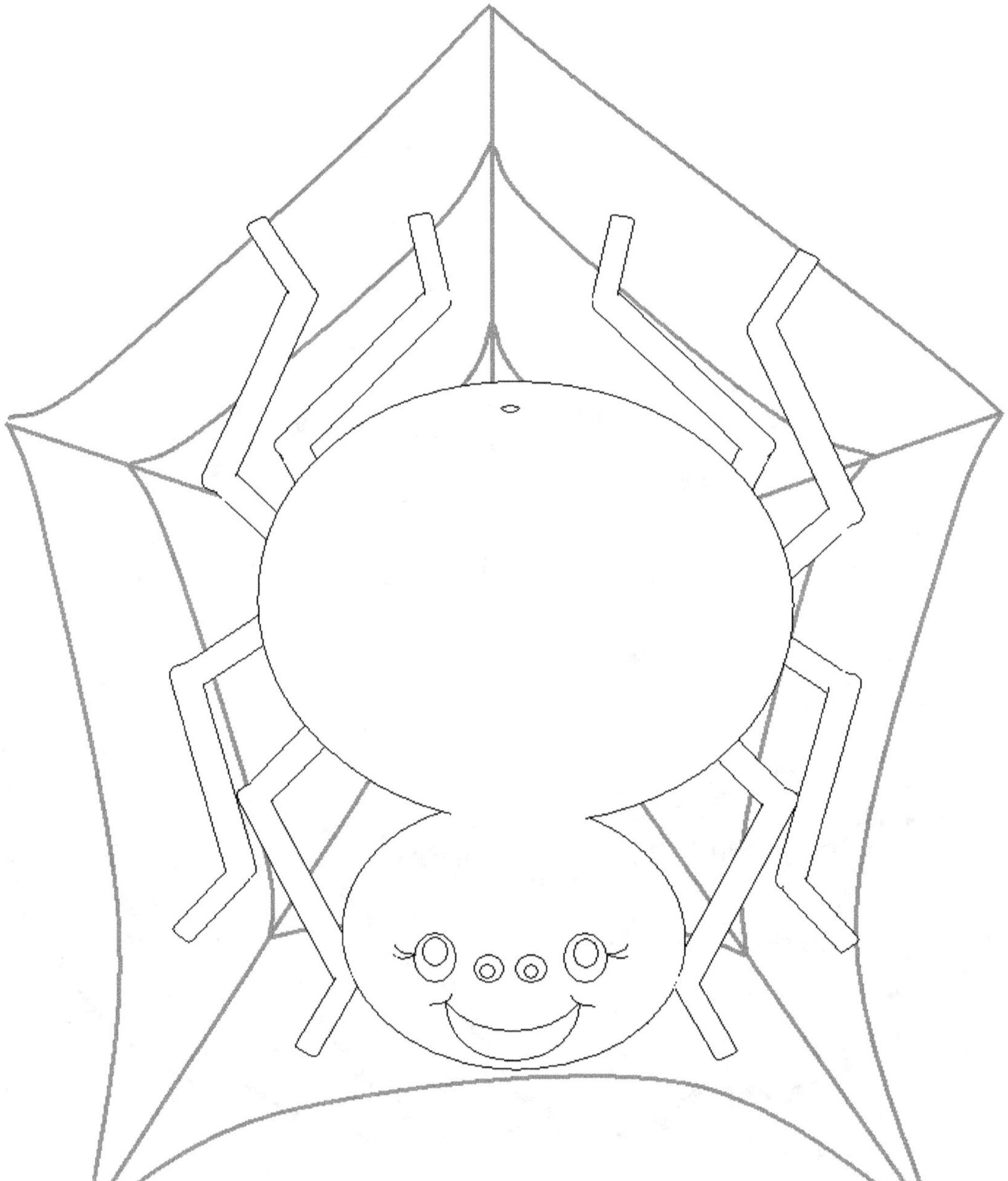

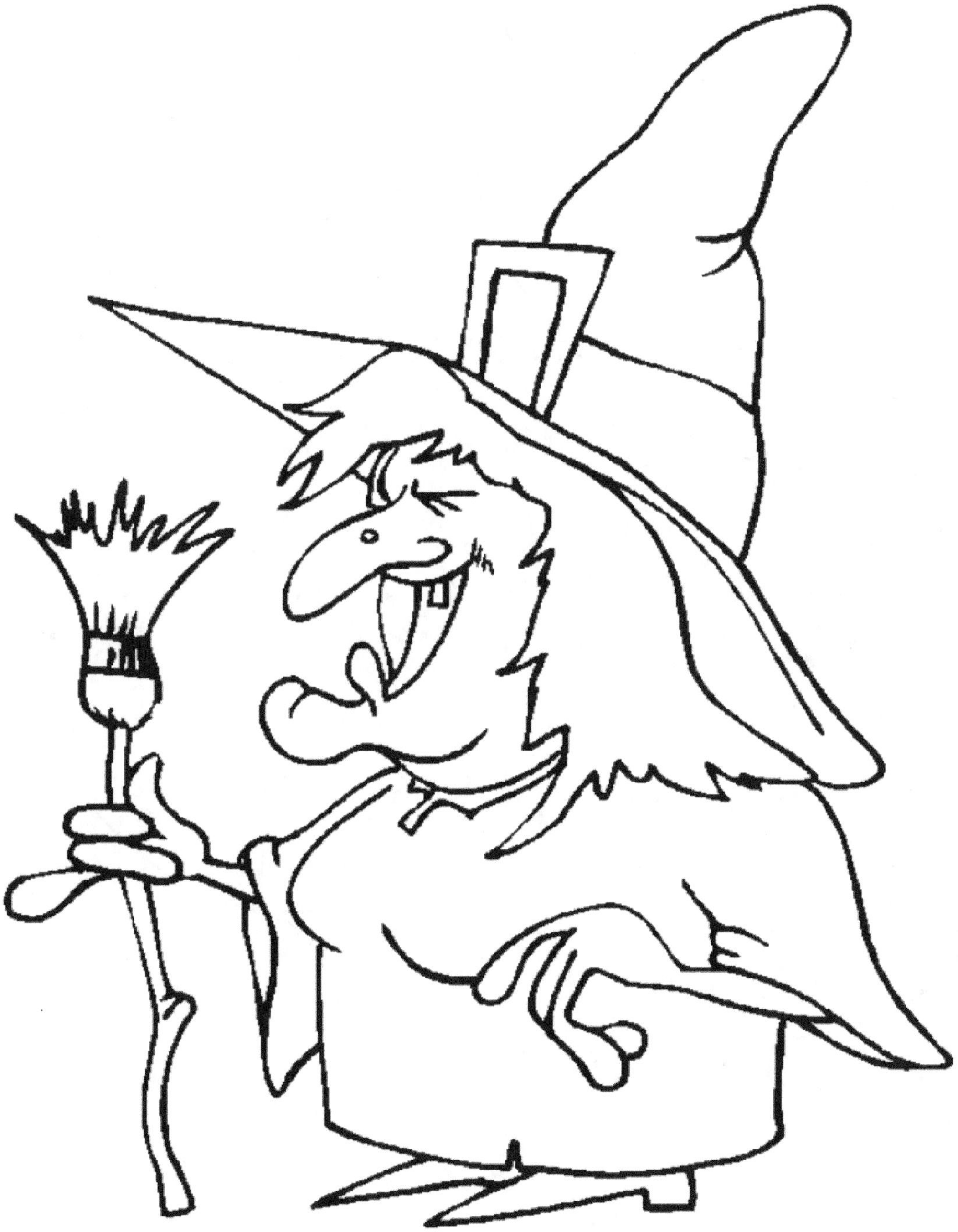

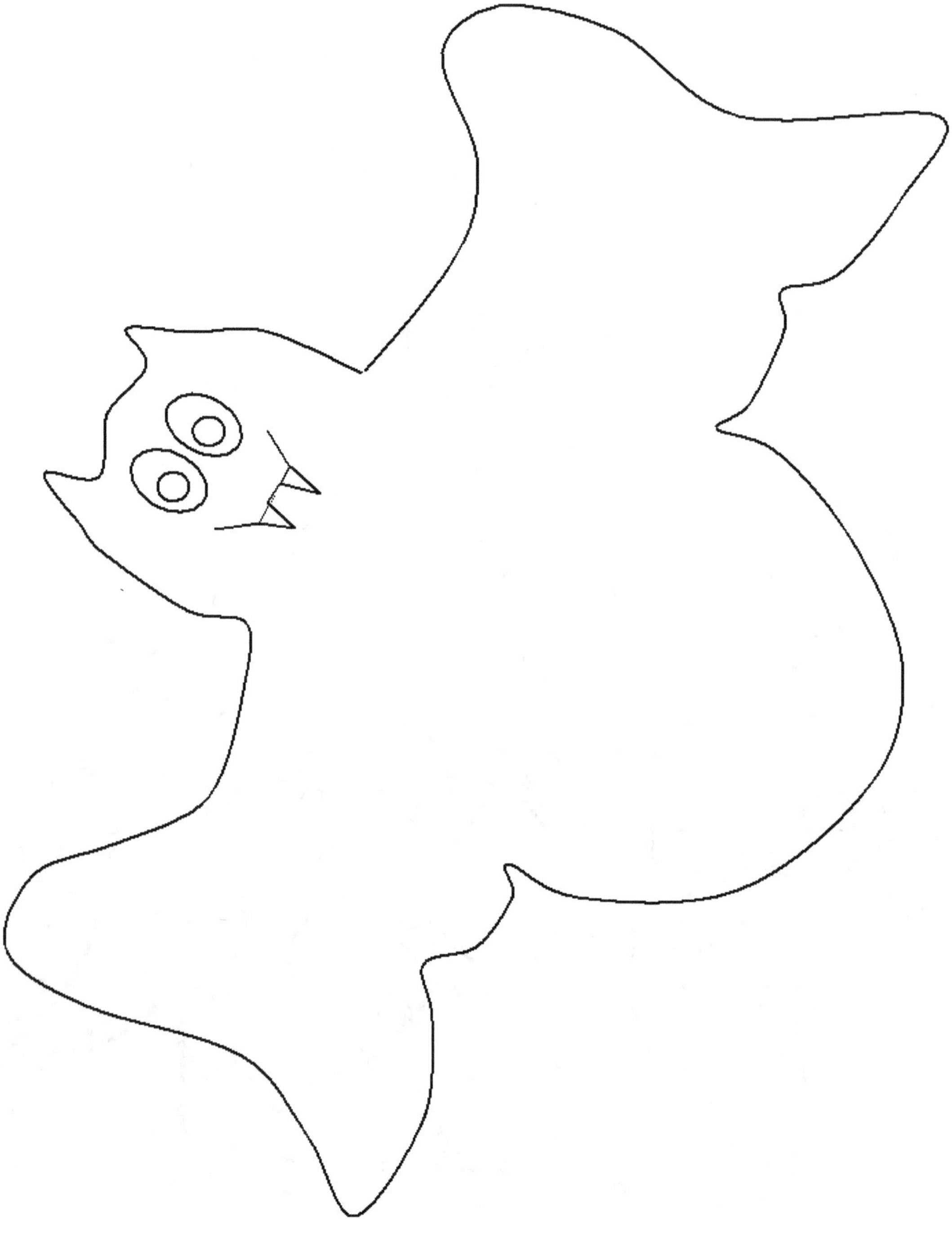

www.ingramcontent.com/pod-product-compliance
Lightning Source LLC
Chambersburg PA
CBHW062206220526
45470CB00009B/2941
* 9 7 8 1 9 7 7 8 1 7 5 2 5 *